DISCOVERING
Your Personality Type

DISCOVERING
Your Personality Type

The Essential Introduction to the Enneagram

••

Revised and Expanded

Don Richard Riso
and Russ Hudson

Houghton Mifflin Company

Boston • New York   2003

FOR A NEW WORLD
BASED ON THE REALIZATION
THAT WE ARE ONE

For information about permission to reproduce selections from this
book, including the *Riso-Hudson Enneagram Type Indicator*, write to
Permissions, Houghton Mifflin Company, 215 Park Avenue South,
New York, New York 10003.

Visit our Web site: www.houghtonmifflinbooks.com.

Library of Congress Cataloging-in-Publication Data
Riso, Don Richard
Discovering your personality type : the essential introduction
to the enneagram / Don Richard Riso and
Russ Hudson.—Rev. and expanded.
p.   cm.
Includes bibliographical references.
ISBN 0-618-21903-X
1. Riso Enneagram Type Indicator. 2. Enneagram.   I. Hudson,
Russ. II. Title
BF698.8.R45R57 2003
155.2'6—dc21   2002191289

If you would like to obtain multiple copies of this book at a
discount, please contact the Special Sales Department at
617-351-5919.

Printed in the United States of America
Book design by Joyce C. Weston

QUM 10 9 8 7 6 5 4 3 2 1

Contents

Acknowledgments
for the Revised and Expanded Edition

When we began writing about the Enneagram, one of our hopes was that publishing books about this wonderful subject would bring us into contact with wonderful people. That hope has come true, and we have been blessed not only with a life's work that seems to us to be worth doing but with extraordinary people with whom to do it.

We have, first of all, to thank those who have come to our Enneagram Workshops and Enneagram Professional Training Programs for their support and enthusiasm. They are spreading word of the Enneagram, quite literally, around the world. We also want to thank those who have encouraged us to develop a questionnaire. It was not something we were particularly interested in doing until we began to appreciate the usefulness of such an instrument. Thus, readers and students alike can perhaps take satisfaction in knowing that they have had an important role in bringing this project about.

Ruth Hapgood, senior editor at Houghton Mifflin, was a wise and steady presence during the years in which we worked together, including the period that saw the first edition of this book into print. We are indebted to her for her unflagging support of our work. Susan Canavan, our current editor, has been a helpful and enthusiastic supporter not only of our work but of the Enneagram. We are grateful to be working with her and look forward to other projects in the future.

Special thanks go to two of our students who are clinical psychologists, Quentin Dinardo, Ph.D., and Betsey Bittlingmaier, Ph.D., for their critique of the first version of this questionnaire. Arlen Baden and Claes Lilja were similarly helpful with comments, critiques, and many useful suggestions. Two other students, William Culp, Ph.D., and David Beswick, made valuable recommendations concerning the instructions for the RHETI that we are continuing to employ in this revised version. We are grateful to everyone who has helped improve the test, including the many students in our workshops and Trainings who so willingly served as "guinea pigs" during the years of its original conception and continued revision.

Walter Geldart, a brilliant Enneagram theoretician and student of ours, has been extremely encouraging and helpful with his comparisons of the RHETI with the MBTI. Walter has also led the way in introducing the Enneagram to the Myers-Briggs community. May his work continue to bear the fruit of cross-fertilization.

Rebecca Xiong has been of great assistance to us and to users of the RHETI by coding it for the Internet so that we could add it to our Web site. The ability to take the RHETI and to have it scored quickly online has enabled this test to be available to many more people, thereby also introducing them to the Enneagram and our work.

Rebecca Newgent, Ph.D. has been extremely helpful through her work in validating the RHETI scientifically. Dr. Newgent validated the RHETI as part of her doctoral work, and her findings have greatly boosted the confidence of those who needed some kind of statistical confirmation that the Enneagram worked and was worthwhile. Of course, we and hundreds of thousands of readers have always felt that intuitively, but it was gratifying to also have our faith confirmed by objective data. We look forward to working with Dr. Newgent — and other qualified researchers — on further validation studies of the RHETI and of other aspects of the Enneagram.

Just as we have thanked our students, we would like to again thank our teachers in the Diamond Approach, Hameed Ali, Alia Johnson, Rennie Moran, Morton Letofsky, Hammed Qabazard, Jeanne Hay, and Kristina Bear for their inspiration, guidance, and unwavering dedication to True Nature.

Russ: thanks to Catherine Chernick, David Fauvre, and Marika Dentai for encouraging me to look more deeply into the three instincts and their interaction with the Enneagram types. They generously shared their own curiosity in this topic which led me to study it more closely myself. I would also like to thank my family for their ongoing support and encouragement.

Don: I would like to offer heartfelt acknowledgment to my mother, Beverly Moreno Pumilia, and my father, Leo Riso. I thank them for all that they have given to me. The older I become, the more I realize how my best qualities are really theirs. Finally, my personal advisors, Brian Lawrence Taylor and Zack, are invaluable in more ways than I can say. Their commitment to my work has been deep and abiding, and without their constant support and guidance, doing it would have been impossible.

Last, we give thanks for the Guidance we have received as we continue to work on the Enneagram and attempt to live its lessons. As much as this work is the product of our own efforts, we can also truly say that it seems to come from something beyond us. There is a consciousness that wishes to manifest itself more clearly in the world — and we believe that the Enneagram is one important expression of this new consciousness. May all those who seek to awaken and know themselves find help with this remarkable tool.

Don Richard Riso and Russ Hudson

Stone Ridge, New York
June 2002

PART ONE

PLEASE NOTE:
If you wish to take the *Riso-Hudson Enneagram Type Indicator* right away, you can go to page 16 in this book now. It is not necessary to know anything about the Enneagram (pronounced "ANY-a-gram") to obtain valid results from this questionnaire.

1. The Multi-Dimensional Enneagram

Understanding Ourselves and Others

The Enneagram is being used daily by millions of people around the world *because it works*. It is the clearest, most accurate method available for understanding ourselves and those who are important to us. It helps us understand why we do not easily get along with certain people while with others we instantly feel that we are old friends. Understanding the Enneagram is like having a pair of special glasses that allows us to see beneath the surface of people with special clarity: we may in fact see them more clearly than they see themselves.

The insights the Enneagram gives us can change our lives, and those who have gotten to know it cannot imagine how they once got along without it. It is as if they had been born color blind and were suddenly able to comprehend the world in all its subtle hues for the first time. They are thrilled to uncover what had been "right in front of their noses" all along but was obscure and hidden from view. The Enneagram opens up whole new vistas for us, new depths of comprehension, new levels of meaning. Knowledge such as this, however, is not obtained without paying a price: there can be no going back to our former blindness once we understand the Enneagram. The world, others, and we will be different forever.

People from diverse cultures all over the world are responding to the Enneagram because they see their experience accurately reflected in it. They are embracing it as one of the most important discoveries of their lives, something that has helped them make sense of what previously seemed impenetrably ambiguous, or worse, utterly chaotic. Once people grasp the essentials of this extraordinary system, they can participate in the noble work of deepening their understanding of themselves and their fellow humans. Who knows what benefits will accrue as new generations are able to draw on the wisdom of the Enneagram throughout their lives?

Moreover, there are as many uses for the Enneagram as there are individuals who use it. Those who are in therapy or in one of the twelve-step programs will find it an invaluable source of insight into their childhood and why they have become the people they are. Spiritual seekers will discover in it a trustworthy guide to the deeper dimensions of human experience. Those of us in intimate relationships will benefit from understanding more about ourselves and our partners. The Enneagram can help us understand what causes our partners to behave in ways that have previously baffled us and can indicate what is needed for more effective communication and conflict resolution. This understanding also helps us bring more acceptance and compassion to our relationships, as well as insight into where and when limits and boundaries need to be set. Learning to understand our partners is the best way to keep a relationship alive and growing. And compassionately understanding ourselves — what *we* need, want, fear, and are afraid of expressing — is the best way to keep our own psyches healthy.

While the Enneagram is primarily a profound psychological and spiritual tool, it is also highly *practical* for business applications because its insights are so on target. Many businesses and organizations are using the Enneagram in management to increase their employees' productivity and, ultimately, their profitability. They have discovered that they can save a great deal of time and frustration for management and employees alike by applying the Enneagram as a communication tool. Corporations have been using the Enneagram for hiring the best possible person for a particular job, for teaching executives to manage their employees more effectively, for customer service, for clarifying a corporate image — a corporate "personality type," so to speak — or for building a more profitable sales force. Team building, executive development, marketing, corporate communication, and conflict resolution — among its many applications — are more effective when insights from the Enneagram are applied in the business world. Major organizations that have been using the Enneagram include Adobe, Amoco, AT&T, Avon Products, Boeing Corporation, The DuPont Company, e-Bay, Prudential Insurance (Japan), General Mills Corporation, General Motors, Alitalia Airlines, KLM Airlines, The Coalition of 100 Black Women, Kodak, Hewlett Packard, Toyota, Procter & Gamble, International Weight Watchers, Reebok Health Clubs, Motorola, and SONY.

What Is the Enneagram?

The Enneagram is a geometric figure that delineates the nine basic personality types of human nature and their complex interrelationships. Each of these nine types has its own way of relating to others, its own set of perceptions and preoccupations, its own values and approaches to life. Each relates to others in different but understandable ways. The Enneagram helps everyone understand that there are nine different points of view, nine distinct sets of values, nine different communication styles, nine ways of solving problems — and so forth — that are all equally useful and valid. All of the types have something necessary to contribute to a thriving, balanced world.

As a typology, the Enneagram helps people recognize and understand overall patterns in human behavior. External behaviors, underlying attitudes, one's characteristic sense of self, conscious and unconscious motivations, emotional reactions, defense mechanisms, object relations, what we pay attention to, our spiritual barriers and potentials — and much more — are all parts of the complex pattern that forms each personality type. While the Enneagram suggests that there are nine basic personality types of human nature, there are, of course, many subtypes and variations within the nine basic categories. Even with all of these subtle distinctions, however, the Enneagram cannot account for every aspect of human nature. Always remember that the Enneagram does not put you in a box — it shows you the box you are already in (but don't know it) and the way out!

Further, while ideas about psychological type cannot tell us everything about people, they help us make meaningful distinctions that are extremely useful. For instance, people generally believe that others think the same way they do. They often believe that others have the same motivations, values, and priorities — although this is usually not the case. However, when personality type is properly understood, communication becomes exponentially more effective because people begin to recognize and make the most of *human diversity*. We learn to respect others who are not the same as we are and to treat them with tolerance and compassion.

How Was the Enneagram Developed?

The Enneagram as a symbol was first brought to the attention of the modern world by the Greek-Armenian spiritual teacher George Ivanovitch Gurdjieff around the turn of the twentieth century. The typology now associated with the symbol was developed by Oscar Ichazo, the founder of the Arica school of self-realization, in the 1950s and 60s. In developing the basic principles of Enneagram theory, Ichazo drew on classic Greek philosophy and ancient spiritual ideas from mystical Judaism and early Christianity. Ichazo taught a number of students the basics of his theories of the Enneagram in Arica, Chile, in 1970, and some of them, notably gestalt psychiatrist Claudio Naranjo, brought the Enneagram to the United States soon thereafter. Within a few years, awareness of this powerful typology had quickly spread around North America. In 1973, Don Riso began developing the Enneagram in the light of modern psychology, adding his own insights and discoveries to the original body of knowledge. He was joined by Russ Hudson in 1988, and both have been writing and teaching about the system ever since.[1]

---

1. For more information about the history and transmission of the Enneagram and about Gurdjieff, Ichazo, and the authors' further development of this system, see *Personality Types, Revised Edition* (11–26) and *The Wisdom of the Enneagram* (19–26). For a discussion of Ichazo's original Enneagram teachings, see *Understanding the Enneagram, Revised Edition* (31–65). Since these books contain full bibliographies about the Enneagram and related topics, that information has not been repeated here.

One central aspect of our work with the Enneagram has been the endeavór to bring our findings into alignment with modern psychological research. In *Understanding the Enneagram*, we saw that the Enneagram adds cohesion and significant insights to the theories of modern psychology with its specificity, comprehensiveness, and elegance (284–311). It organizes observations about human nature by consolidating what has already been discovered as well as by suggesting new avenues for investigation. By "cleaving the diamond" of the psyche along its proper internal lines, the Enneagram presents us with the categories that we actually find in everyday life. What is particularly intriguing is that this system, based on ancient philosophical ideas and empirical observations, anticipates many of the findings of the *Diagnostic and Statistical Manual of Mental Disorders,* fourth edition (the DSM-IV), of the American Psychiatric Association and other typologies.

What Creates Our Enneagram Type?

One of the primary things to understand about the Enneagram is that we find ourselves reflected in the whole of it. From one point of view, the personality types are metaphors for the various psychological functions operating in each of us. (See Chapter 7 for more on the Functions.) We develop into one of the nine personality types because our consciousness has developed in certain ways as a result of our heredity and childhood experiences. Nevertheless, our personality type is largely inborn and is the result of what psychologists call *temperament.* Any woman who has been a mother is aware that children are quite distinct from one another even when they are still in the womb.[2] The child then uses the strengths of his or her temperament as a primary way to cope with stresses in his or her environment. But in the process of

2. Retired Stanford psychiatrist David Daniels has noted that a study done by Alexander Thomas, M.D., and Stella Chess, M.D., at New York University School of Medicine, with no knowledge of the Enneagram, isolated nine basic patterns of temperament in infants through experimental means. This landmark study is called the New York Longitudinal Study.

adapting, a variety of unconscious mechanisms and structures come into play that help the child feel safe but that also limit his or her sense of identity. In a sense, the development of the personality is as much a defense against our early environment as it is an adaptive reaction to it. The remaining eight personality types (which we develop to greater or lesser degrees throughout our lives) represent the other potentials of our psyche and are important parts of who we are.

How the Enneagram Helps Us Grow

But how does a system of personality types help us liberate ourselves? Aren't we more than a simple type? The answer is yes we are. Human beings are complex and mysterious, but in fact, our *personalities* are based primarily on repetitive habits and patterns. Our personalities are not the whole of our psyches, although they are enormously important in that they largely affect the way we see the world and interact with it. Thus, the personality is a kind of filter that potentially limits us and our freedom.

By indicating the chief features and barriers of our psychic landscape, the Enneagram can help us prepare for a more profoundly direct and spiritual relationship with reality. While many people are interested in living more spirit-centered lives, many of us have not had the time or opportunity to develop a reliable practice of meditation or self-observation. Nor do most of us have access to an authentic spiritual school that could guide us along our path.

The Enneagram can help us prepare ourselves for the inward journey by showing us many of the obstacles as well as supports available within our own psyches. It can help us see the reason for taking time from daily routines to meditate or practice spiritual disciplines so that we can acquire the resources necessary for our transformation and liberation.

In the process of teaching the Enneagram to thousands of people for many years, we have seen over and over that the key to transformation lies in our capacity to be *present* — to be deeply abiding in the here and now, with our minds, hearts, and bodies fully engaged. While this seems an obvious and simple thing, there is one huge barrier to our being more conscious and attuned in the present moment. It is *that our personality is not at all interested in being here and now.*

In fact, the personality is always drawing us somewhere else, even if we think of ourselves as realistic, practical people. Our habitual thoughts, emotional reactions, fantasies about the future, and old stories about who we are and what others have done to us cloud our awareness and limit our capacity to be fully awake and present to reality. But it is all the more difficult to break out of our old patterns because we are almost totally unaware of them. *The mechanisms of our personality are invisible to us.* We therefore need to find a way to awaken to our true condition, and having awakened, to remain mindful of the siren-calls of personality.

The amazing thing is that as we are able to bring a nonjudgmental awareness to the reactivity of our personality, our perceptions become sharper, and we begin to discover a vast part of ourselves that is not conflicted, self-deluding, or fearful. As we become more conscious of the mechanical aspects of our personality (that is, our automatic, reactive, defensive patterns), we are less and less controlled by them. By using the habits of our personality to remind us to be present, and then *remaining* present while observing and feeling the reactions and habits of the personality, we gradually open to real freedom and inner peace. Thus, the paradox of the Enneagram is this: *we study the Enneagram because it is necessary to become conscious of how our personality operates so that we can become free of it.*

The Real Purpose of the Enneagram

While it is extremely valuable to discover our dominant type, it is best to not get distracted by typing and to keep in mind the real purpose of the Enneagram. First, remember that we have the whole Enneagram within us. When we speak of our type it is useful to think of it as our *dominant* type — our default setting and motivational core. This is an extremely valuable thing to know, and it can greatly facilitate our growth by being aware of what is most centrally driving our ego agendas. That being said, we will manifest characteristics from all of the nine types from time to time. In short, we are all nine types.

Second, remember that the reason we learn our Enneagram type is to remind us to come back to the present moment when we see our personality drawing our attention into its particular preoccupations and reactions. When we use our knowledge of the types this way, they become liberating rather than constricting us in old identities. As important as discovering our type is, a much more significant achievement is to be willing to observe it in action. Indeed, discovering our personality type only presents us with this greater challenge of courageously observing ourselves as we really are, no matter what we find. Without the willingness to see the maneuvers of our personality from moment to moment, transformation cannot take place. Unless we learn to observe ourselves, finding our type (with the Enneagram or any other system) will give us little more than another label with which we can hide from ourselves. If we only find our type but go no further, the Enneagram itself can become an obstacle to our growth.

Third, it is in the act of seeing ourselves objectively that something lets go in us: a new possibility is created when we allow the grace available in the moment to touch us. We discover that at our deepest *we are not our personality.* When we experience this truth, transformation becomes possible. Without our trying to do anything to "fix" ourselves, the act of bringing awareness to the moment causes our higher essential qualities to become more available and our personality to lose its grip over us. As we have more moments of freedom from our personality, our essence reveals its many facets — acceptance, love, authenticity, forgiveness, compassion, courage, joy, strength, and presence — as well as gratitude, vitality, and boundlessness — and all of the other manifestations of the human spirit. By moving beyond merely knowing our type to the ability to see ourselves as we are, the shift from personality to essence takes place and we discover that we can live differently. We discover that we can be free.

In the end, the Enneagram can be thought of as a treasure map that indicates where the secret riches of the innermost self can be discovered. Pointing out each type's path to self-realization is thus one of the Enneagram's most profound gifts. But the Enneagram is only a map, and it is up to us to make the journey: only we can accept the daily challenge and adventure that is our life. The Enneagram takes us to the threshold of spirit and freedom, love and liberation, self-surrender and self-actualization. Once we have arrived at that uncharted land, we will begin to recognize our truest self, the self beyond personality, the self of essence. That self, of course, cannot be tested by a questionnaire, but only by life itself.

The Riso-Hudson Enneagram Type Indicator

If we are going to use the Enneagram for self-understanding, for relationships, or for practical applications, we must be able to accurately assess our dominant personality type (as well as those of others). The questionnaire in this book, the *Riso-Hudson Enneagram Type Indicator* (RHETI, version 2.5), is a reliable tool for that purpose. Those who are already acquainted with the Enneagram have intuitively sensed that this system works; the RHETI attempts to complement intuition by verifying the personality types empirically. If the Enneagram is to become more widely known, its intuitive validity will have to be corroborated by hard evidence. This questionnaire is offered as a step toward the scientific validation of the Enneagram as a whole.[3]

Scientific Validation and Limitations with Psychological Tests

The intention behind developing the RHETI was not merely to give people a shortcut for determining their personality type. If the Enneagram is to continue to gain mainstream and academic acceptance, the empirical validation of this system is necessary, and having a reliable questionnaire is essential. That process was

---

3. Qualified psychometric researchers are invited to contact the authors to conduct further validation studies of the RHETI and of the Enneagram. See our contact page at the end of this book.

boosted by the first independent validation of this test — a recognized standard in the field — and will be accelerated with further validation studies and subsequent developments of the test.

But an Enneagram questionnaire — indeed, any questionnaire that aims to help us discover our personality type — cannot provide real and complete self-knowledge by itself. At best, all an Enneagram test can do is to provide evidence about your dominant type. While we have done our best to make the RHETI as valid and reliable an instrument as possible, it is good to remember some of the limitations inherent in using a test to determine your Enneagram type.

Some limitations are inherent in the nature of any test that relies on self-reporting. No such test can be foolproof or 100 percent accurate. After several years of experience with test construction, we have come to the conclusion (supported by studies in psychometrics) that it is virtually impossible to devise a questionnaire that is over 85–90 percent accurate, and any claims to anyone's having done so should be met with skepticism. In the appendix of this book, we have included the results of an academic study of the RHETI administered independently by Rebecca Newgent, Ph.D., as her doctoral dissertation at the University of Akron. We intend to use this study to make further refinements of the test, and hope that it will lead to further validation studies of the RHETI.[3] In any case, Dr. Newgent's findings were highly encouraging and placed the RHETI well within the range of a viable psychological test.

But even with sufficient reliability in a test's construction, other challenges remain. One of the primary limitations with any personality test based on self-reporting is that it takes some degree of self-knowledge to take a type-test, yet this is often the very thing that is in short supply. Because many people lack self-knowledge, they are at a loss about what is true about them when a questionnaire asks them to report on their attitudes or behaviors. At the heart of the problem is the fact that each of us has a certain self-image that does not include everything about us. For example, we may be far more aggressive than we realize, or we may not be as sensitive, loving, dependable, or outgoing as our self-image leads us to believe. One of the values of the Enneagram is to help us correct our distorted notions about ourselves — but until we can acknowledge our "blind spots," we will not be able to recognize them either in ourselves or in a test.

It is also in the very nature of certain personality types to have difficulty identifying themselves. The three primary types — Threes, Sixes, and Nines — probably have the most trouble because their identity depends on their identifications with others. They live through others or else live through the real or imagined reactions of others to them. Either way, because they do not see themselves directly, testing for these types is more difficult. Of course, all of the types present other problems caused by self-deception, self-justification, and the desire to "look good." This can be particularly true when the test is administered in the workplace. People are likely to respond in ways that they believe are expected of them rather than as they truly feel.

Of course there are other pitfalls in any self-scored test: people can skip questions or entire pages, or they can make mistakes in arithmetic as they add their scores. Sometimes they do not understand the vocabulary, do not read or follow the instructions, or get impatient and answer the questions arbitrarily. Other errors are more subtle: while some respondents do not have the self-knowledge to answer the questions appropriately, others may know the Enneagram types so well that they are able to skew the answers to make the test confirm the type that they *want* to be. Others may overanalyze the questions and become confused by hair-splitting and thinking of fantastic situations in which both of the statements might possibly be true of them. When one considers all of the potential sources of error that can be introduced in test-taking, it is a wonder that psychological tests, including the RHETI, ever come out at all.

Despite these problems, the RHETI has proven to range from about 56–82 percent accurate for determining the basic personality type (depending on the type). While carefully reading Enneagram books and going to workshops is probably the most reliable way to identify or confirm one's dominant type, many people like to get launched on this journey of self-discovery by having an accurate personality type indicator available. At the very least, tests can be useful in narrowing down the possibilities from nine to two or three. In the last analysis, finding your dominant type ultimately depends on honest self-observation over time.

Insights obtained from a test, workshop, book, or an Enneagram teacher should be used only as corroborative pieces of evidence in the process of self-discovery. It is unwise to expect any method to be the only way to discover our dominant type. The responsibility for finding out who we are always lies with us. Insights from any method should be considered along with all the other available evidence before we come to any final conclusions. Talking to friends, reading the descriptions of the types, attending workshops, and above all, relying on your own self-observation over a period of time are the best ways to discover your type with confidence.

Differences Between the Earlier Version of *Discovering Your Personality Type* and This New Third Edition

While the earlier two versions of this book have proven to be favorites with Enneagram readers, we realized that people were primarily purchasing them for the test and not using much of the supportive text on interpretation. At the same time, we were aware of the need for a simple, fresh introduction to the nine Enneagram types for people newly acquainted with the system. Further, we had made some additional changes and refinements to the version of the test in the last edition of *Discovering Your Personality Type* (version 2.0), resulting in the more accurate version 2.5 that is included here. It was also version 2.5 that was studied and scientifically validated.

Thus, it made sense to release a new edition of this book with the validated version of the test and with additional introductory material. Our hope was that readers would find in this newest edition all they needed to begin their exploration of the Enneagram without going into the greater complexities and subtleties of the system that we have described in our other works.

As a result, we removed some of the extra interpretive material and replaced it with fuller introductions to the nine types as well as to the basics of the system. The two-paragraph descriptions of the nine types from the last edition are here replaced with treatments of over 2,500 words each. In this new edition, readers can take the test and immediately go to the type chapters for an introduction to all the most important points they need to know about their type. We have also included new material for more advanced students so that those familiar with our other books will be well rewarded by investigating the type chapters and other sections in this edition.

2. Instructions for the RHETI

The *Riso-Hudson Enneagram Type Indicator* consists of 144 paired statements. It is a forced-choice test: it requires you to choose the statement in each pair that describes you best. In certain pairs, you may feel that neither describes you very well or, conversely, that both statements are *almost equally true*. Nevertheless, you must try to choose the statement that describes you best.

You can take the RHETI several different ways, although we have found that the most accurate approach is to take the test from the point of view of the past, *as you have been most of your life.* (This does not mean to take it as you were in childhood, but rather, as you were as a young adult.)

Mark an X in the box to the right of the statement you have selected. For example, if you feel that a statement such as "I have preferred oranges" fits you better than "I have preferred apples," draw an X in the box to the right of the first statement. You may, of course, have not liked either oranges or apples, or you may have liked both. But if you were forced to choose between the two, which would you choose? Select the statement that reflects your lifelong attitudes and behavior better than the other. (If, for example, you have preferred apples most of your life, but now prefer oranges, choose the apples statement.)

This is especially true if you have been in psychological or spiritual work and feel that you have changed over time. If you have changed significantly, it is important to identify what you were like *before* the changes in your personality took place. While it is possible to think of exceptions, don't overthink the choices. Go with your gut impulse and with the general trends.

Be sure to choose one statement for each of the 144 pairs, taking care to put an X in the correct box. To help, a dotted line has been drawn from the end of each statement to its corresponding box in the columns on the right of the page.

You may find that there are five to ten pairs of statements for which the choice is particularly difficult. The statements in the RHETI are for making subtle distinctions between the personality types, and choosing one over the other requires you to carefully consider which response is more true of you. In some of the pairs, both statements may *almost* be equally true of you. If you reflect carefully, however, you will find that one of the statements is more true than the other. Choose this statement in each pair.

Remember that there are no "right" answers. This instrument is attempting to discover your basic personality type, and if several of your selections are actually "wrong," they will not, in general, undermine the results of the test. So-called incorrect responses will more likely occur with factors other than those involving your basic personality type. This is why the degree of falsification they introduce in the test will be relatively small. To ensure the test's overall accuracy, however, it is essential that you answer honestly and thoughtfully, choosing the statement in each pair that best reflects your attitudes and feelings. Optimally, you should choose one of the statements in all 144 pairs; however, if there are a few pairs in which you are absolutely certain that neither statement fits you, leave them blank. Please be careful, however, not to skip over those statements which you merely find difficult to answer. It is useful to wrestle with difficult statements; you can skip only those few that you feel are totally irrelevant to you.

It is also important to note that the RHETI is not attempting to ascertain whether you are mentally healthy or unhealthy. A diagnosis such as this is beyond the scope of this test. So you can relax while taking the test. All of the questions are gauged to the average range of human behavior and are not designed to reveal psychological problems.

You may want to skip particularly difficult pairs and return to them after you have finished the entire test. Or you may wish to review your choices for the whole test after you have gone through it once. Feel free to change an original response if, after further reflection, you feel that another response is more appropriate. Naturally, you must guard against attempting to "fix" the results toward one type or another. But, because of nervousness, resistance, or other factors, you may not be able to answer some of the questions on a first pass through the test. If so, please review your responses.

The profile you get from the RHETI will reflect your personality's principal psychological functions, the balance of which changes over time. While your basic personality type should remain the same, other personality functions shift as you grow, change attitudes, experience stress, and so forth. You may find it informative to take the RHETI on several occasions to see what changes occur in your profile. You might also, for instance, take it first as you were in the past, then, answering in a different color of ink or pencil, take the test again *as you are now in the present.* As just noted, the RHETI should indicate that your basic type is the same, although the profile produced by the balance of the other types as Functions (see Chapter 15) will be somewhat different.

If you have difficulty discerning your dominant type because two or more top scores are very close, you might also find it helpful to discuss your choices with someone who knows you well, such as a spouse, close friend, or therapist. You may also ask someone else to take the RHETI for you as an external observer, answering the questions as he or she sees you. This approach, from the point of view of how others see us, can be particularly illuminating. Further, you can have your spouse, close friend, or therapist take the test for you, as if they were you. This method will also yield valuable results and likely be the occasion for a stimulating conversation. Several scoring sheets have been provided at the end of the test so that you or others can take it on different occasions or in different ways. Taking and grading the RHETI will require approximately forty-five minutes to an hour.

After you have taken the *Riso-Hudson Enneagram Type Indicator,* read the corresponding type chapters provided in Part Two to confirm your results. (Also see *Personality Types, Understanding the Enneagram,* and *The Wisdom of the Enneagram* for more information and complete — but different — descriptions.)

Remember that the primary goal of this test is to determine your dominant personality type; in some cases, it may be necessary to interpret the results to account for unusual findings. For guidelines about interpreting the RHETI, see the section on Interpretation following the test and scoring pages.

Please note! The accuracy of this questionnaire will be increased if you understand that, in a sense, we have four "selves": our past self, our present self, our ideal self, and our self as others see us. **The RHETI is attempting to discern only your past self.** It is therefore essential to maintain the focus of your answers *on your past self only,* and not to mix responses from your past self with your present, ideal, or social self. (The RHETI also includes a few questions that ask how we think or believe others see us. However, these questions should also be answered from the point of view of your past self.)

3. The *Riso-Hudson Enneagram Type Indicator* (Version 2.5)

	A	B	C	D	E	F	G	H	I
1. I've been romantic and imaginative.					[ ]				
I've been pragmatic and down-to-earth	[ ]								
2. I have tended to take on confrontations								[ ]	
I have tended to avoid confrontations.	[ ]								
3. I have typically been diplomatic, charming, and ambitious			[ ]						
I have typically been direct, formal, and idealistic.				[ ]					
4. I have tended to be focused and intense.								[ ]	
I have tended to be spontaneous and fun-loving									[ ]
	A	B	C	D	E	F	G	H	I
SUBTOTAL									

	A	B	C	D	E	F	G	H	I

5. I have been a hospitable person and have enjoyed welcoming new friends into my life. . . . . [ ] *(F)*
   I have been a private person and have not mixed much with others . . . . [ ] *(E)*

6. It's been difficult for me to relax and stop worrying about potential problems . . . . [ ] *(C)*
   It's been difficult for me to get myself worked up about potential problems . . . . [ ] *(A)*

7. I've been more of a "street-smart" survivor . . . . [ ] *(G)*
   I've been more of a "high-minded" idealist . . . . [ ] *(D)*

8. I have needed to show affection to people. . . . . [ ] *(F)*
   I have preferred to maintain some distance with people . . . . [ ] *(H)*

9. When presented with a new experience, I've usually asked myself if it would be useful to me . . . . [ ] *(C)*
   When presented with a new experience, I've usually asked myself if it would be enjoyable . . . . [ ] *(I)*

	A	B	C	D	E	F	G	H	I

	A	B	C	D	E	F	G	H	I
10. I have tended to focus too much on myself.					[ ]				
I have tended to focus too much on others.	[ ]								
11. Others have depended on my insight and knowledge									[ ]
Others have depended on my strength and decisiveness.								[ ]	
12. I have come across as being too unsure of myself		[/]							
I have come across as being too sure of myself				[ ]					
13. I have been more relationship-oriented than goal-oriented.						[ ]			
I have been more goal-oriented than relationship-oriented.			[ ]						
14. I have not been able to speak up for myself very well					[ ]				
I have been outspoken — I've said what others wished they had the nerve to say									[ ]
	A	B	C	D	E	F	G	H	I

A	B	C	D	E	F	G	H	I

15. It's been difficult for me to stop considering alternatives and do something definite . . . . [ ] (H)
It's been difficult for me to take it easy and be more flexible . . . . [ ] (E)

16. I have tended to be careful and hesitant . . . . [ ] (B)
I have tended to be bold and domineering . . . . [ ] (H)

17. My reluctance to get too involved has gotten me into trouble with people . . . . . . [ ] (A)
My eagerness to have people depend on me has gotten me into trouble with them . . . . [ ] (G)

18. Usually, I have been able to put my feelings aside to get the job done . . . . [ ] (D)
Usually, I have needed to work through my feelings before I could act . . . . [ ] (F)

19. Generally, I've been methodical and cautious . . . . [ ] (B)
Generally, I've been adventurous and taken risks . . . . [ ] (I)

A	B	C	D	E	F	G	H	I

	A	B	C	D	E	F	G	H	I

20. I have tended to be a supportive, giving person who seeks intimacy with others . . . . [ ] (G)

I have tended to be a serious, reserved person who likes discussing issues . . . . [ ] (D)

21. I've often felt the need to be a "pillar of strength" . . . . [ ] (H)

I've often felt the need to perform perfectly . . . . [ ] (C)

22. I've typically been interested in asking tough questions and maintaining my independence . . . . [ ] (I)

I've typically been interested in maintaining my stability and peace of mind . . . . [ ] (A)

23. I've been a bit cynical and skeptical . . . . [ ] (B)

I've been a bit mushy and sentimental . . . . [ ] (F)

	A	B	C	D	E	F	G	H	I

	A	B	C	D	E	F	G	H	I
24. I've often worried that I'm missing out on something better									[·]
I've often worried that if I let down my guard, someone will take advantage of me							[·]		
25. My habit of being "stand-offish" has annoyed people					[·]				
My habit of telling people what to do has annoyed people				[·]					
26. I have tended to get anxious if there was too much excitement and stimulation	[·]								
I have tended to get anxious if there wasn't enough excitement and stimulation									[·]
27. I have depended on my friends and they have known that they can depend on me			[·]						
I have not depended on people; I have done things on my own			[]						
	A	B	C	D	E	F	G	H	I

	A	B	C	D	E	F	G	H	I

28. I have tended to be detached and preoccupied . . . . [ ] (H)
    I have tended to be moody and self-absorbed . . . . [ ] (E)

29. I have liked to challenge people and "shake them up" . . . . [ ] (G)
    I have liked to comfort people and calm them down . . . . [ ] (F)

30. I have generally been an outgoing, sociable person . . . . [ ] (I)
    I have generally been an earnest, self-disciplined person . . . . [ ] (D)

31. I've wanted to "fit in" with others — I get uncomfortable when I stand out too much . . . . [ ] (A)
    I've wanted to stand out from others — I get uncomfortable when I don't distinguish myself . . . . [ ] (C)

	A	B	C	D	E	F	G	H	I

	A	B	C	D	E	F	G	H	I

32. Pursuing my personal interests has been more important to me than having stability and security . . . . [✓] (H)
    Having stability and security has been more important to me than pursuing my personal interests. . . . . [ ] (A)

33. When I've had conflicts with others, I've tended to withdraw . . . . [ ] (F)
    When I've had conflicts with others, I've rarely backed down . . . . [✓] (G)

34. I have given in too easily and let others push me around . . . . [ ] (A)
    I have been too uncompromising and demanding with others. . . . . [✓] (D)

35. I've been appreciated for my unsinkable spirit and resourcefulness. . . . . [ ] (I)
    I've been appreciated for my deep caring and personal warmth. . . . . [ ] (F)

	A	B	C	D	E	F	G	H	I

	A	B	C	D	E	F	G	H	I
36. I have wanted to make a favorable impression on others....................			[]						
I have cared little about making a favorable impression on others									[]
37. I've depended on my perseverance and common sense.........................		[]							
I've depended on my imagination and moments of inspiration					[]				
38. Basically, I have been easy-going and agreeable.......	[]								
Basically, I have been hard-driving and assertive							[]		
39. I have worked hard to be accepted and well-liked			[]						
Being accepted and well-liked has not been a high priority for me				[]					
40. In reaction to pressure from others, I have become more withdrawn...................								[]	
In reaction to pressure from others, I have become more assertive.........................									[]
	A	B	C	D	E	F	G	H	I

	A	B	C	D	E	F	G	H	I

41. People have been
interested in me because
I've been outgoing,
engaging, and interested
in them . . . . [ ] (F)
People have been
interested in me because
I've been quiet, unusual,
and deep . . . . [ ] (E)

42. Duty and responsibility
have been important
values for me . . . . [ ] (B)
Harmony and acceptance
have been important
values for me . . . . [ ] (A)

43. I've tried to motivate
people by making big
plans and big promises . . . . [ ] (G)
I've tried to motivate
people by pointing out the
consequences of not
following my advice . . . . [ ] (E)

44. I have seldom been
emotionally demonstrative . . . . [ ] (H)
I have often been
emotionally demonstrative . . . . [ ] (E)

	A	B	C	D	E	F	G	H	I

	A	B	C	D	E	F	G	H	I

45. Dealing with details has not been one of my strong suits . . . . [ ] (I)
    I have excelled at dealing with details . . . . [ ] (C)

46. I have often emphasized how different I am from most people, especially my family . . . . [ ] (E)
    I have often emphasized how much I have in common with most people, especially my family . . . . [ ] (A)

47. When situations have gotten heated, I have tended to stay on the sidelines . . . . [ ] (H)
    When situations have gotten heated, I have tended to get right into the middle of things . . . . [ ] (G)

48. I have stood by my friends, even when they have been wrong . . . . [ ] (C)
    I have not wanted to compromise what is right, even for friendship . . . . [ ] (D)

	A	B	C	D	E	F	G	H	I

	A	B	C	D	E	F	G	H	I
49. I've been a well-meaning supporter						[]			
I've been a highly-motivated go-getter			[]						
50. When troubled, I have tended to brood about my problems						[]			
When troubled, I have tended to find distractions for myself									[]
51. Generally, I've had strong convictions and a sense of how things should be					[]				
Generally, I've had serious doubts and have questioned how things seemed to be								[]	
52. I've created problems with others by being pessimistic and complaining		[]							
I've created problems with others by being bossy and controlling							[]		
53. I have tended to act on my feelings and let the "chips fall where they may"						[]			
I have tended not to act on my feelings lest they stir up more problems	[]								
	A	B	C	D	E	F	G	H	I

	A	B	C	D	E	F	G	H	I

54. Being the center of
attention has usually felt
natural to me . . . . [ ] (C)
Being the center of
attention has usually felt
strange to me . . . . [ ] (E)

55. I've been careful and
have tried to prepare for
unforeseen problems . . . . [ ] (A)
I've been spontaneous
and have preferred to
improvise as problems
come up . . . . [ ] (I)

56. I have gotten angry when
others have not shown
enough appreciation for
what I have done for them . . . . [ ] (F)
I have gotten angry when
others have not listened
to what I have told them . . . . [ ] (C)

57. Being independent and
self-reliant has been
important to me . . . . [ ] (G)
Being valued and admired
has been important to me. . . . . [ ] (C)

	A	B	C	D	E	F	G	H	I

	A	B	C	D	E	F	G	H	I

58. When I've debated with friends, I've tended to press my arguments forcefully . . . . [ ]
When I've debated with friends, I've tended to let things go to prevent hard feelings. [ ]

59. I have often been possessive of loved ones — I have had trouble letting them be . . . . [ ]
I have often "tested" loved ones to see if they were really there for me . . . . [ ]

60. Organizing resources and making things happen has been one of my major strengths. . . . . [ ]
Coming up with new ideas and getting people excited about them has been one of my major strengths . . . . [ ]

61. I've tended to be driven and very hard on myself . . . . [ ]
I've tended to be too emotional and rather undisciplined . . . . [ ]

	A	B	C	D	E	F	G	H	I

	A	B	C	D	E	F	G	H	I

62. I have tried to keep my life fast-paced, intense, and exciting. . . . . [ ] (I)
I have tried to keep my life regular, stable, and peaceful . . . . [ ] (A)

63. Even though I've had successes, I've tended to doubt my abilities . . . . [ ] (B)
Even though I've had setbacks, I've had a lot of confidence in my abilities . . . . [ ] (C)

64. I generally have tended to dwell on my feelings and to hold onto them for a long time. . . . . [ ] (F)
I generally have tended to minimize my feelings and not pay very much attention to them . . . . [ ] (H)

65. I have provided many people with attention and nurturance . . . . [ ] (F)
I have provided many people with direction and motivation. . . . . [ ] (G)

	A	B	C	D	E	F	G	H	I

	A	B	C	D	E	F	G	H	I
66. I've been a bit serious and strict with myself				[]					
I've been a bit free-wheeling and permissive with myself									[]
67. I've been self-assertive and driven to excel			[]						
I've been modest and have been happy to go at my own pace	[]								
68. I have been proud of my clarity and objectivity								[]	
I have been proud of my reliability and commitment		[]							
69. I have spent a lot of time looking inward — understanding my feelings has been important to me					[]				
I have not spent much time looking inward — getting things done has been important to me							[]		
70. Generally, I have thought of myself as a sunny, casual person	[]								
Generally, I have thought of myself as a serious, dignified person				[]					
	A	B	C	D	E	F	G	H	I

	A	B	C	D	E	F	G	H	I
71. I've had an agile mind and boundless energy									[ ]
I've had a caring heart and deep dedication						[ ]			
72. I have pursued activities that had a substantial potential for reward and personal recognition			[ ]						
I have been willing to give up reward and personal recognition if it meant doing work I was really interested in.								[ ]	
73. Fulfilling social obligations has seldom been high on my agenda.					[ ]				
I have usually taken my social obligations very seriously		[ ]							
74. In most situations, I have preferred to take the lead.								[ ]	
In most situations, I have preferred to let someone else take the lead	[ ]								
	A	B	C	D	E	F	G	H	I

	A	B	C	D	E	F	G	H	I

75. Over the years, my values
and lifestyle have changed
several times. [ ] (C)
Over the years, my values
and lifestyle have
remained fairly consistent . . . . [ ] (D)

76. Typically, I have not had
much self-discipline. . . . . [ ] (I)
Typically, I have not had
much connection with
people. . . . . [ ] (H)

77. I have tended to withhold
my affection and have
wanted others to come
into my world . . . . [ ] (E)
I have tended to give my
affection too freely and
have wanted to extend
myself to others. . . . . [ ] (F)

78. I have had a tendency to
think of worst-case
scenarios . . . . [ ] (C)
I have had a tendency to
think that everything will
work out for the best . . . . [ ] (A)

	A	B	C	D	E	F	G	H	I

	A	B	C	D	E	F	G	H	I

79. People have trusted me because I am confident and can look out for them . . . . [ ] (G)
People have trusted me because I am fair and will do what is right . . . . [ ] (D)

80. Often, I have been so involved in my own projects that I have become isolated from others . . . . [ ] (H)
Often, I have been so involved with others that I have neglected my own projects . . . . [ ] (F)

81. When meeting someone new, I have usually been poised and self-contained . . . . [ ] (C)
When meeting someone new, I have usually been chatty and entertaining . . . . [ ] (I)

82. Generally speaking, I have tended to be pessimistic . . . . [ ] (E)
Generally speaking, I have tended to be optimistic . . . . [ ] (A)

83. I have preferred to inhabit my own little world . . . . [ ] (H)
I have preferred to let the world know I'm here . . . . [ ] (G)

	A	B	C	D	E	F	G	H	I

	A	B	C	D	E	F	G	H	I

84. I have often been troubled by nervousness, insecurity, and doubt. . . . . [ ]
I have often been troubled by anger, perfectionism, and impatience . . . . [ ]

85. I realize that I have often been too personal and intimate . . . . [ ]
I realize that I have often been too cool and aloof . . . . [ ]

86. I have lost out because I have not felt up to taking opportunities . . . . [ ]
I have lost out because I have pursued too many possibilities . . . . [ ]

87. I have tended to take a long time to get into action . . . . [ ]
I have tended to get into action quickly . . . . [ ]

88. I usually have had difficulty making decisions . . . . . . [ ]
I seldom have had difficulty making decisions . . . . [ ]

	A	B	C	D	E	F	G	H	I

	A	B	C	D	E	F	G	H	I

89. I have had a tendency to come on a little too strong with people . . . . [ ] (F)
I have had a tendency not to assert myself enough with people . . . . [ ] (A)

90. Typically, I have been even-tempered . . . . [ ] (C)
Typically, I have had strong changes of mood . . . . [ ] (F)

91. When I've been unsure of what to do, I've often sought the advice of others . . . . [ ] (B)
When I've been unsure of what to do, I've tried different things to see what worked best for me . . . . [ ] (I)

92. I have worried that I would be left out of others' activities . . . . [ ] (F)
I have worried that others' activities would distract me from what I had to do . . . . [ ] (C)

93. Typically, when I have gotten angry, I have told people off . . . . [ ] (G)
Typically, when I have gotten angry, I have become distant . . . . [ ] (C)

	A	B	C	D	E	F	G	H	I

	A	B	C	D	E	F	G	H	I

94. I've tended to have trouble
falling asleep . . . . [ ] (H)
I've tended to fall asleep
easily . . . . [ ] (A)

95. I have often tried to figure
out how I could get closer
to others . . . . [ ] (F)
I have often tried to figure
out what others want from
me. . . . . [ ] (B)

96. I have usually been
measured, straight-talking,
and deliberate . . . . [ ] (G)
I have usually been
excitable, fast-talking,
and witty . . . . [ ] (I)

97. Often, I have not spoken
up when I've seen others
making a mistake . . . . [ ] (E)
Often, I have helped others
see that they are making a
mistake . . . . [ ] (D)

	A	B	C	D	E	F	G	H	I

A	B	C	D	E	F	G	H	I

98. During most of my life, I
have been a stormy person
who has had many volatile
feelings. . . . . [ ]
During most of my life, I
have been a steady person
in whom "still waters
run deep". . . . . [ ]

99. When I have disliked
people, I have usually
tried hard to stay cordial
— despite my feelings. . . . . [ ]
When I have disliked
people, I have usually let
them know it — one way
or another . . . . [ ]

100. Much of my difficulty
with people has come
from my touchiness and
taking everything too
personally. . . . . [ ]
Much of my difficulty
with people has come
from my not caring about
social conventions . . . . [ ]

101. My approach has been to
jump in and rescue people. . . . . [ ]
My approach has been to
show people how to help
themselves. . . . . [ ]

A	B	C	D	E	F	G	H	I

	A	B	C	D	E	F	G	H	I

102. Generally, I have enjoyed "letting go" and pushing the limits . . . . [ ] (I)

Generally, I have not enjoyed losing control of myself very much . . . . [ ] (D)

103. I've been overly concerned with doing better than others . . . . [ ] (C)

I've been overly concerned with making things okay for others . . . . [ ] (A)

104. My thoughts generally have been speculative — involving my imagination and curiosity . . . . [ ] (H)

My thoughts generally have been practical — just trying to keep things going . . . . [ ] (C)

105. One of my main assets has been my ability to take charge of situations . . . . [ ] (G)

One of my main assets has been my ability to describe internal states . . . . [ ] (E)

	A	B	C	D	E	F	G	H	I

	A	B	C	D	E	F	G	H	I

106. I have pushed to get things done correctly, even if it made people uncomfortable . . . . [ ] (D)
I have not liked feeling pressured, so I have not liked pressuring anyone else . . . . [ ] (A)

107. I've often taken pride in how important I am in others' lives . . . . [ ] (H)
I've often taken pride in my gusto and openness to new experiences. . . . . [ ] (I)

108. I have perceived that I've often come across to others as presentable, even admirable. . . . . [ ] (C)
I have perceived that I've often come across to others as unusual, even odd. . . . . [ ] (H)

109. I have mostly done what I had to do . . . . [ ] (C)
I have mostly done what I wanted to do . . . . [ ] (E)

	A	B	C	D	E	F	G	H	I

	A	B	C	D	E	F	G	H	I
110. I have usually enjoyed high-pressure, even difficult, situations.							[]		
I have usually disliked being in high-pressure, even difficult, situations.	[]								
111. I've been proud of my ability to be flexible — what's appropriate or important often changes				[]					
I've been proud of my ability to take a stand — I've been firm about what I believe in					[]				
112. My style has leaned toward spareness and austerity.								[]	
My style has leaned toward excess and overdoing things.									[]
113. My own health and well-being have suffered because of my strong desire to help others						[]			
My relationships have suffered because of my strong desire to attend to my personal needs.					[]				

A	B	C	D	E	F	G	H	I

	A	B	C	D	E	F	G	H	I

114. Generally speaking, I've
    been too open and naive . . . . . . [ ] (A)
    Generally speaking, I've
    been too wary and guarded . . . . . . [ ] (B)

115. I have sometimes put
    people off by being too
    aggressive . . . . [ ] (H)
    I have sometimes put
    people off by being too
    "uptight" . . . . [ ] (E)

116. Being of service and
    attending to the needs of
    others has been a high
    priority for me . . . . [ ] (F)
    Finding alternative ways
    of seeing and doing things
    has been a high priority
    for me . . . . [ ] (H)

117. I've been single-minded
    and persistent in
    pursuing my goals . . . . [ ] (C)
    I've preferred to explore
    various courses of action
    to see where they lead . . . . [ ] (I)

A	B	C	D	E	F	G	H	I

	A	B	C	D	E	F	G	H	I

118. I have frequently been drawn to situations that stir up deep, intense emotions. . . . . [ ] (E)
I have frequently been drawn to situations that make me feel calm and at ease . . . . [ ] (A)

119. I have cared less about practical results than about pursuing my interests. . . . . [ ] (I)
I have been practical and have expected my work to have concrete results. . . . . [ ] (G)

120. I have had a deep need to belong . . . . [ ] (C)
I have had a deep need to feel balanced . . . . [ ] (E)

121. In the past, I've probably insisted on too much closeness in my friendships. . . . . [ ] (I)
In the past, I've probably kept too much distance in my friendships. . . . . [ ] (C)

	A	B	C	D	E	F	G	H	I

	A	B	C	D	E	F	G	H	I
122. I've had a tendency to keep thinking about things from the past					[]				
I've had a tendency to keep anticipating things I'm going to do									[]
123. I've tended to see people as intrusive and demanding								[]	
I've tended to see people as disorganized and irresponsible				[]					
124. Generally, I have not had much confidence in myself		[]							
Generally, I have had confidence only in myself								[]	
125. I've probably been too passive and uninvolved	[]								
I've probably been too controlling and manipulative							[]		
126. I've frequently been stopped in my tracks by my self-doubt					[]				
I've rarely let self-doubt stand in my way			[]						
	A	B	C	D	E	F	G	H	I

A	B	C	D	E	F	G	H	I

127. Given a choice between something familiar and something new, I've usually chosen something new . . . . [ ]
I've generally chosen what I knew I already liked: why be disappointed with something I might not like? . . . . [ ]

128. I have given a lot of physical contact to reassure others about how I feel about them . . . . [ ]
I have generally felt that real love does not depend on physical contact . . . . [ ]

129. When I've needed to confront someone, I've often been too harsh and direct . . . . [ ]
When I've needed to confront someone, I've often "beaten around the bush" too much . . . . [ ]

A	B	C	D	E	F	G	H	I

	A	B	C	D	E	F	G	H	I

130. I have been attracted to subjects that others would probably find disturbing, even frightening. . . . . [ ] (H)
I have preferred not to spend my time dwelling on disturbing, frightening subjects . . . . [ ] (A)

131. I have gotten into trouble with people by being too intrusive and interfering . . . . [ ] (G)
I have gotten into trouble with people by being too evasive and uncommunicative . . . . [ ] (C)

132. I've worried that I don't have the resources to fulfill the responsibilities I've taken on . . . . [ ] (G)
I've worried that I don't have the self-discipline to focus on what will really fulfill me. . . . . [ ] (I)

133. Generally, I've been a highly intuitive, individualistic person. . . . . [ ] (F)
Generally, I've been a highly organized, responsible person. . . . . [ ] (D)

	A	B	C	D	E	F	G	H	I

	A	B	C	D	E	F	G	H	I

134. Overcoming inertia has been one of my main problems . . . . [ ]
Being unable to slow down has been one of my main problems . . . . [ ]

135. When I've felt insecure, I've reacted by becoming arrogant and dismissive . . . . [ ]
When I've felt insecure, I've reacted by becoming defensive and argumentative . . . . [ ]

136. I have generally been open-minded and willing to try new approaches . . . . [ ]
I have generally been self-revealing and willing to share my feelings with others . . . . [ ]

137. I've presented myself to others as tougher than I really am . . . . [ ]
I've presented myself to others as caring more than I really do . . . . [ ]

A	B	C	D	E	F	G	H	I

	A	B	C	D	E	F	G	H	I

138. I usually have followed
my conscience and reason . . . . [ ]
I usually have followed
my feelings and impulses . . . . [ ]

139. Serious adversity has
made me feel hardened
and resolute . . . . [ ]
Serious adversity has
made me feel discouraged
and resigned . . . . [ ]

140. I usually have made sure
that I had some kind
of "safety net" to fall
back on . . . . [ ]
I usually have chosen to
live on the edge and to
depend on others as little
as possible . . . . [ ]

141. I've had to be strong for
others, so I haven't had
time to deal with my
feelings and fears . . . . [ ]
I've had difficulty coping
with my feelings and
fears, so it's been hard for
me to be strong for others . . . . [ ]

A	B	C	D	E	F	G	H	I

	A	B	C	D	E	F	G	H	I

142. I have often wondered why people focus on the negative when there is so much that's wonderful about life . . . . [ ] (A)

I have often wondered why people are so happy when so much in life is messed up . . . . [ ] (C)

143. I have tried hard not to be seen as a selfish person . . . . [ ] (G)

I have tried hard not to be seen as a boring person . . . . [ ] (I)

144. I have avoided intimacy when I feared I would be overwhelmed by people's needs and demands . . . . [ ] (H)

I have avoided intimacy when I feared I would not be able to live up to people's expectations of me . . . . [ ] (C)

	A	B	C	D	E	F	G	H	I

4. Scoring Instructions

Add the X's marked in Column A, Column B, Column C, and so forth, through Column I. Place the number of X's you made in the boxes below for columns A through I. If you marked one box in each pair of statements and have added the number of X's correctly, the sum will be 144. If not, go back and recheck for mistakes either in counting X's or in arithmetic.

Each column corresponds to a personality type, as given below. Please note that they are *not* in numerical order.

Columns	A	B	C	D	E	F	G	H	I
Numerical Values									
Personality Type	Nine	Six	Three	One	Four	Two	Eight	Five	Seven

Mark the proper numerical values on one of the score sheets on the following pages. Note that the personality types have been arranged *in numerical order* beginning with types Two, Three, and Four (in *The Feeling Triad*), and so forth. Connect the marks you have made to produce a graph that represents the various values for the nine Functions within your personality. (For more about interpreting the Functions in your full personality profile, see Chapter 15.) The second score sheet is for analyzing your scores according to The Hornevian Groups (see *Personality Types, Revised Edition,* 433–36). These Groups indicate whether the overall orientation of your personality is assertive, dutiful, or withdrawn. Note that the columns on this score sheet have been reorganized for these three Groups.

Except in unusual circumstances (discussed in the Interpretation section) your highest score will indicate your basic type, or it will almost certainly be among the top three scores. To confirm your results, read the complete descriptions in Part Two of this book or in *Personality Types* and *Understanding the Enneagram.*

If properly taken, the *Riso-Hudson Enneagram Type Indicator* will accurately assess your basic personality type. If the results you obtain are unclear, please review your responses to see if, on further reflection, you wish to change any of them.

An alternative method for discovering your personality type is to have one or more people who know you well take the RHETI as if they were answering the test for you (as mentioned in the Instructions section). This method tests how others see you; if their results and yours are the same (at least for the basic type), you can be reassured that the RHETI has discriminated your type accurately. On the other hand, a finding of a different basic type (or of a dramatically different pattern for the other eight types) could be the basis for discussing various dimensions of your personality that you formerly may have been unaware of.

The median score is 16 for each type. If the Functions of your personality were in perfect balance, you would score 16 on each of the nine types. This result is extremely rare, and it is normal to have wide variations from the median. Some scores will fall below the median; some will be above it. Further, the test scores represent your overall personality pattern at a particular time in your life. This pattern reveals which aspects of your life are getting the most attention from you. The "above average" and "below average" as well as the "high" and "low" ranges indicated on the score sheets are not to be interpreted as indications of pathology or as value judgments. They are only indicators of the *relative* development of the various functions within your personality. Thus, those functions that are already developed probably do not need to be emphasized further, while you may want to give more attention to those with lower scores.

After you have plotted your scores on the score sheet(s), read the appropriate description of your type in Part Two, and then go to Part Three for more information about interpreting your results.

Score Sheet I: The Three Triads

Type	Two	Three	Four	Five	Six	Seven	Eight	Nine	One	
Score										
32										
31										
30										
29										
28										
27	X									
26					X					
25										
24										High
23					X					
22	X						X			
21			X							
20										Above Average
19			X							
18						X			X	
17		X						X	X	
16			+			+				Median
15										
14		X			X					
13			X	X						
12								+	X	Below Average
11										
10						X				
9				X			X			
8				+					X	Low
7										
6										
5										
4							X			
3										
2						X				
1										
Type	Two	Three	Four	Five	Six	Seven	Eight	Nine	One	

	The Feeling Triad			The Thinking Triad			The Instinctive Triad		

5⁄0   58   54   39   70   24⁄29

Score Sheet I: The Three Triads

Type	Two	Three	Four	Five	Six	Seven	Eight	Nine	One	
Score										
32										
31										
30										
29										
28										
27										
26										
25										
24										High
23										
22										
21							X			
20	X					X				Above Average
19									X	
18										
17		X			X					
16										Median
15										
14										
13			X							
12					X					Below Average
11				X						
10								X		
9										
8				X						Low
7										
6										
5										
4										
3										
2										
1										
Type	Two	Three	Four	Five	Six	Seven	Eight	Nine	One	
	The Feeling Triad			The Thinking Triad			The Instinctive Triad			

Score Sheet II: The Hornevian Grops

Type	Three	Seven	Eight	One	Two	Six	Four	Five	Nine	
Score										
32										
31										
30										
29										
28										
27										
26										
25										
24										High
—										
23										
22										
21										
20										Above Average
—										
19										
18										
17										
16										Median
—										
15										
14										
13										
12										Below Average
—										
11										
10										
9										
8										Low
—										
7										
6										
5										
4										
3										
2										
1										
Type	Three	Seven	Eight	One	Two	Six	Four	Five	Nine	

The Assertive Group Sum = _____	The Dutiful Group Sum = _____	The Withdrawn Group Sum = _____

Score Sheet II: The Hornevian Grops

Type	Three	Seven	Eight	One	Two	Six	Four	Five	Nine	
Score										
32										
31										
30										
29										
28										
27										
26										
25										
24	- - -	- - -	- - -	- - -	- - -	- - -	- - -	- - -	- - -	High
—										
23										
22										
21										
20	- - -	- - -	- - -	- - -	- - -	- - -	- - -	- - -	- - -	Above Average
—										
19										
18										
17										
16	- - -	- - -	- - -	- - -	- - -	- - -	- - -	- - -	- - -	Median
—										
15										
14										
13										
12	- - -	- - -	- - -	- - -	- - -	- - -	- - -	- - -	- - -	Below Average
—										
11										
10										
9										
8	- - -	- - -	- - -	- - -	- - -	- - -	- - -	- - -	- - -	Low
—										
7										
6										
5										
4										
3										
2										
1										
Type	Three	Seven	Eight	One	Two	Six	Four	Five	Nine	
	The Assertive Group Sum = _____			The Dutiful Group Sum = _____			The Withdrawn Group Sum = _____			

PART TWO

PART TWO

5. How the System Works

The following explanation covers most of the basics that you will need to understand how the Enneagram works. We hope it will be especially helpful for beginners, although there is material here for advanced students, too. As you will see, only a few simple concepts are needed to get started. This system ultimately becomes subtle and complex, as you will appreciate the more you use it in your life.[1]

Structure

The Enneagram's structure may look complicated, although it is actually simple. It will help you understand the Enneagram if you sketch it yourself.

Draw a circle and mark nine equidistant points on its circumference. Designate each point by a number from one to nine, with nine at the top, for symmetry and by convention. Each point represents one of the nine basic personality types.

The nine points on the circumference are also connected with each other by inner lines. Note that points Three, Six, and Nine form an equilateral triangle. The remaining six points are connected in the following order: One connects with Four, Four with Two, Two with Eight, Eight with Five, Five with Seven, and Seven with One. These six points form an irregular hexagram. The meaning of these inner lines will be discussed shortly.

---

1. For more guidelines, consult *Personality Types*, 27–55, and for further clarifications, see *Understanding the Enneagram*, 11–30.

The Enneagram

Your Basic Personality Type

From one point of view, the Enneagram can be seen as a set of nine distinct personality types, with each number on the Enneagram denoting one type. It is common to find a little of yourself in all nine of the types, although one of them should stand out as being closest to yourself. This is your *basic personality type.*

We all emerge from childhood with *one* of the nine types dominating our personality, with inborn temperament and other prenatal factors being the main determinants of our type. This is one area where most all of the major Enneagram authors agree — *we are born with a dominant type.* Subsequently, this inborn orientation largely determines the ways in which we learn to adapt to our early childhood environment. By the time children are four or five years old, their consciousness has developed sufficiently to have a separate sense of self. Although their identity is still very fluid, at this age children begin to establish themselves and find ways of fitting into the world on their own. Thus, the overall orientation of our personality reflects the totality of all childhood factors (including genetics) that influenced its development. (For more about the developmental patterns of each personality type, see the related section in the type descriptions in *Personality Types* and in *The Wisdom of the Enneagram.* There is a discussion of the overall childhood developmental theory in *Understanding the Enneagram,* 67–70.)

Several more points can be made about the basic type itself.

1) People do not change from one basic personality type to another. Of course, we may change and develop over time and learn new coping skills, but the foundation of our personality — what we initially developed from — remains the same.

2) The descriptions of the personality types are universal and apply equally to males and females, since no type is inherently masculine or feminine.

3) Not everything in the description of your basic type will apply to you all the time because you fluctuate constantly among the healthy, average, and unhealthy traits that make up your personality type.

4) The Enneagram uses *numbers* to designate each of the types because numbers are value neutral — they imply the whole range of attitudes and behaviors of each type without specifying anything either positive or negative. Unlike the labels used in psychiatry, numbers provide an unbiased, shorthand way of indicating a lot about a person without being pejorative or highlighting pathology.

5) The numerical ranking of the types is not significant. A larger number is no better than a smaller number; it is not better to be a Nine than a Two just because nine is a bigger number.

6) No type is inherently better or worse than any other. While all the personality types have unique assets and liabilities, some types are often more desirable than others in any given culture or group. Furthermore, for one reason or another, you may not be happy being a particular type. You may feel that your type is "handicapped" in some way. As you learn more about all the types, you will see that just as each has unique capacities, each has different limitations. If some types are more esteemed in Western society than others, it is because of the qualities that society rewards, not because of any superior value of those types. The ideal is to become *your best self*, not to imitate the assets of another type.

Identifying Your Basic Personality Type

If taken properly, the RHETI will identify your basic personality type for you. This short section is included so that we can have a basic understanding of all the types here without referring to the longer descriptions in the next section.

As you think about your personality, which of the following nine roles fits you best most of the time?

**The Enneagram with
Riso-Hudson Type Names**

These one-word descriptors can be expanded into four-word sets of traits. Keep in mind that these are merely highlights and do not represent the full spectrum of each type. If you were to describe yourself in a few words, which of the following word clusters would come closest?

Type One, ***the Reformer,***
   is principled, purposeful, self-controlled, and perfectionistic.
Type Two, ***the Helper,***
   is generous, demonstrative, people-pleasing, and possessive.
Type Three, ***the Achiever,***
   is adaptable, excelling, driven, and image-conscious.
Type Four, ***the Individualist,***
   is expressive, dramatic, self-absorbed, and temperamental.

Type Five, **the Investigator,**
  is perceptive, innovative, secretive, and isolated.
Type Six, the **Loyalist,**[2]
  is engaging, responsible, anxious, and suspicious.
Type Seven, **the Enthusiast,**
  is spontaneous, versatile, distractible, and scattered.
Type Eight, **the Challenger,**
  is self-confident, decisive, willful, and confrontational.
Type Nine, **the Peacemaker,**
  is receptive, reassuring, accommodating, and complacent.

The Triads

The Enneagram is a three-by-three arrangement of nine personality types *in three Triads*. There are three types in the *Instinctive Triad*, three in the *Feeling Triad*, and three in the *Thinking Triad*, as shown below. Each Triad consists of three personality types that have in common the assets and liabilities of that Triad. For example, personality type Four has unique strengths and liabilities involving its feelings, which is why it is in the Feeling Triad. Likewise, the Eight's assets and liabilities involve its relationship to its instinctual drives, which is why it is in the Instinctive Triad, and so forth for all nine personality types.

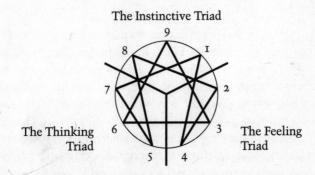

The Triads of the Enneagram

---

2. We also call Type Six "The Troubleshooter."

The inclusion of each type in its Triad is not arbitrary. Each type results from a particular relationship with a cluster of issues that characterize that Triad. Most simply, these issues revolve around a powerful, largely unconscious emotional response to the loss of contact with the core of the self. In the Instinctive Triad, the underlying emotion is *anger* or *rage*. In the Feeling Triad, the emotion is *shame*, and in the Thinking Triad, it is *anxiety* or *dread*. Of course, all nine types contain all three of these fundamental emotional reactions, but in each Triad, the personalities of the types are particularly affected by that Triad's emotional theme.

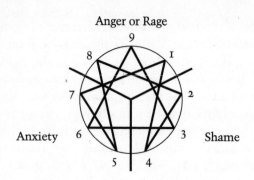

Dominant Emotion in Each Triad

Further, each type has a particular way of coping with the dominant emotional theme of its Triad. In the Instinctive Triad, **Eights** act out their anger and instinctual energies. In other words, when Eights feel anger building in them, they immediately respond to it in some physical way — raising their voices, moving more forcefully, and so forth. Others can clearly see that Eights are angry because they give themselves permission to assert their anger, vitality, and instinctual energy directly and physically. **Nines** deny their anger and instinctual energies as if to say, "What anger? I am not a person who gets angry." Nines are the type most out of touch with their anger and instinctual energies, often feeling threatened by them. Of course, Nines get angry like everyone else, but they try to stay out of their darker feelings by focusing on idealizations of their relationships and their world. **Ones** attempt to control or repress their anger and instinctual energy. They feel that they must stay in control of themselves, especially of their angry feelings and instinctual impulses at all times. They would like to direct these energies according to the dictates of their highly developed inner critic (superego), the source of their strictures on themselves and others.

In the Feeling Triad, **Twos** attempt to compensate for their underlying shame by getting other people to like them and to want them in their lives. They also want to convince *themselves* that they are good and loving by focusing on their positive feelings for others while repressing their negative feelings (such as resentment at not being appreciated enough). As long as Twos can get positive emotional responses from others, they feel wanted and thus have value. **Threes** try to *deny* their shame and are potentially the most out of touch with underlying feelings of inadequacy. Threes learn to cope with shame by trying to become what they believe a valuable, successful person is like. Thus, Threes learn to perform well, to be acceptable, even outstanding, and are often driven relentlessly in their pursuit of success as a way of staving off feelings of shame and fears of failure. **Fours** attempt to avoid their underlying shame by focusing on how unique and special their particular talents, feelings, and personal characteristics are. Fours focus on their individuality and creativity as a way of dealing with their shameful feelings, although Fours are the type most likely to succumb to feelings of inadequacy. Fours also manage their shame by cultivating a rich, romantic fantasy life in which they do not have to deal with whatever in their life seems drab or ordinary to them.

In the Thinking Triad, **Fives** have anxiety about the outer world and about their capacity to cope with it. Thus, they cope with their fear by withdrawing from the world. Fives become secretive, isolated loners who use their minds to penetrate into the nature of reality. Fives hope that eventually, as they understand reality on their own terms, they will be able to rejoin the world and participate in it, but they never feel they know enough to participate with total confidence. Instead, they involve themselves with increasingly complex *inner* worlds. *Sixes* are the most anxious type and the most out of touch with their own sense of inner knowing and confidence. Unlike Fives, Sixes have trouble trusting their own minds, so they are constantly looking outside themselves for something to make them feel sure of themselves. They might turn to philosophies, beliefs, relationships, jobs, savings, authorities, or any combination of the above. But no matter how many security structures they create, Sixes still feel doubtful and anxious. They may even begin to doubt the very people and beliefs that they have turned to for reassurance. Sixes may also respond to their anxiety by impulsively confronting it — defying their fear in the effort to be free of it. *Sevens* have anxiety about their *inner* world. There are feelings of pain, loss, deprivation, and the general anxiety that Sevens would like to avoid as much as possible. To cope with these feelings, Sevens keep their minds occupied with exciting possibilities and options — as long as they have something stimulating to anticipate, Sevens feel that they can distract themselves from their fears. Sevens, in most cases, do not stop merely at thinking about these options, however. As much as possible, they attempt to actually realize as many of their options as they can. Thus, Sevens can be found staying on the go, pursuing one experience after another, and keeping themselves entertained and engaged with their many ideas and activities.

Going with or Against the Dominant Emotion

Since the Enneagram was first taught in America in 1970, the system seemed to have one type that was an exception to all the others — type Six. It was observed that Sixes apparently came in *two* different styles: the phobic Six and the counterphobic Six. In other words, some Sixes (phobics) tended to cave in to their anxiety, feeling timid, weak, and self-doubting, while others (counterphobics) went against their anxiety, in a bold and defiant assertion against whatever they were afraid of. While this distinction seemed to be true, it presented a curious problem. Why would eight of the types manifest in only one way, while one type — the

Six — has two major versions of itself? Wasn't this coming very close to indicating that there are really ten types?

As we looked more closely at the psychology of type Six, and interviewed many people of this type in our workshops and training programs, it became obvious that most Sixes had some mixture of both phobic and counterphobic traits. They were overwhelmed by some fears, while aggressively defying others. Further, we noted that a person could not be counterphobic unless he was already more fundamentally phobic: a person cannot go against a fear that he or she does not have. This explained the Six, while still leaving the question of why the Six alone would have this dual characteristic.

To solve this dilemma, some Enneagram authors have argued that there is a *counterpassion* version of each type. They felt that there might be "counterenvy" Fours and "countergluttony" Sevens, but this seemed to us to be an unwieldy solution and to introduce unnecessary confusion to the system. It also led to mistyping. We met some Sevens, for instance, who felt that they were cheerful, outgoing "counterenvy" Fours. This made little sense, considering that Fours are melancholic and withdrawn by definition. But eventually a simpler solution presented itself to us.

We realized that *the types in each Triad are always either going with or against the dominant emotion of the Triad*. The idea of a "counter" movement in each type like the "counterphobic" movement in type Six applies not to the Passion (gluttony, pride, vanity, envy, etc.) but to the underlying emotional reaction of each Triad. In the case of the Six, both the passion and the dominant emotion of the Triad are the same — fear, which is probably why this phenomenon was first noticed in the Six. But *in all three* of the Thinking Triad types (Five, Six, and Seven) in which the dominant emotion is fear, we can see phobic and counterphobic traits and reactions.

For instance, *Fives* express their counterphobia by focusing on subjects that frighten them. Many Fives enjoy reading, or even writing, horror stories. Other Fives who feared insects as children grew up to go against their fears by becoming entomologists, studying insects for a living. Those fearing disease or the sight of blood might become cancer researchers or pathologists, and so forth. Yet, the same Fives might be phobic in other areas, feeling overwhelmed and paralyzed by other anxieties: they might become anxious in crowded places or become terrified at the prospect of going on a date. *Sevens* are clearly more naturally counterphobic as their personality "default" setting. Their very desire to keep busy and stimulated can be seen as a counterphobic move to control their anxieties. But we also see a phobic side in them: the fear of being afraid, of not having the "nerve" to do something. They are especially phobic about being quiet and allowing whatever is in their unconscious to arise into their awareness. Sevens are afraid of the darkness inside themselves, and their hyperactivity is a reaction against that.

Similarly, types Eight, Nine, and One in the Instinctive Triad can be seen as either *going with or against their anger* — the dominant emotion of the Instinctive Triad. All of these types are either giving in to their anger and frustration and openly expressing it in various ways, or finding ways to suppress it, to hold it in check. *Eights* are fairly comfortable about expressing their rage, but there are also Eights who attempt to conquer their rage as a sign of superiority and self-control. Further, Eights may also go through periods during which they simply shut down and grow numb, using drugs and alcohol, television, or other distractions to repress their anger and other intense feelings. *Nines* are more clearly on the side of suppressing their rage and anger, but there are also Nines who act out rage and can be violent as part of their job or in sports. After suppressing their anger for long periods of time, most Nines eventually have blowups in which they rage over seemingly insignificant problems. Other Nines will give themselves license to express their anger in seething sarcasm or criticism. *Ones* are often visibly angry but tend to deny it. Many Ones try to go against their anger by attempting to control it, by keeping a close watch on their reactions, and by tensing their bodies against any instinctual impulses — especially toward anger. Of course, Ones can never be completely successful in controlling themselves, and they express their rage in outbursts of temper, rants and tirades of various sorts, as well as sarcasm and put-downs. Thus, we could describe behaviors in all three of these types as having both anger and "counteranger" elements. But here, resisting their anger is not the same as working through or resolving it, any more than the Thinking types' counterphobic reactions resolve their underlying anxiety.

Lastly, the three Feeling types, Two, Three, and Four, *either go with or against their shame* — the dominant emotion of their Triad. Two, Three, and Four have periods of their lives in which they collapse into their shame, feeling deficient and empty. At other times, these types inflate their sense of worth to feel superior or important. *Twos* are either riddled with feeling needy and rejected by others, or defending against these feelings by inflating their importance in others' lives. ("Where would they be without me?") Twos also alternate between the feeling of being excluded and unwanted and feeling that they are more loving than anyone else around them — that others depend on their deeper love. *Threes* tend to express the "countershame" elements of their personality more often, particularly in public. The Three's drive for success and narcissistic demand for positive attention can be seen as a countershame characteristic. But privately, Threes are prone to falling into periods of intense self-rejection, feeling ashamed of themselves and feeling a deep sense of inner deficiency. *Fours* are more obviously prone to collapsing into their shame and self-doubt, but may also defend against these feelings with an exaggerated view of their talents and significance. ("No one recognizes what a creative genius I am.") While each type in this Triad is unique, the overall shame/inflation pattern is the same. The types of the Feeling Triad alternate between collapsing into shame and deficiency or going against these feelings by exaggerating their positive qualities. Again, the narcissistic inflation of these types is a defense against their shame, and not a genuine working-through or resolution of it.

Thus, we find that type Six is not unique after all. Each of the nine Enneagram types can be seen to fluctuate between being driven by the dominant underlying emotion of its Triad or reacting against it in an unconscious way. As the types become more unhealthy, the extremes of these polarities grow even more extreme. Thinking types become both more phobic and counter-phobic, Instinctive types become more raging and shut down, and Feeling types become more shame-filled and narcissistically grandiose. Thus, we can see that the solution is not for Thinking types to deny their fear, for Instinctive types to deny their anger, or for Feeling types to deny their shame. The real resolution of all of these polarities lies *in being present repeatedly with the dominant emotion of your Triad with patience, truthfulness, and compassion.*

The Wing

No one is a pure personality type: everyone is a unique mixture of his or her basic type and usually *one* of the two types adjacent to it on the circumference of the Enneagram. One of the two types adjacent to your basic type is called your *wing.*

Your basic type dominates your overall personality, while the wing complements it and adds important, sometimes contradictory, elements to your total personality. Your wing is the "second side" of your personality, and it must be taken into consideration to better understand yourself or someone else. For example, if you are a personality type Three, you will likely have either a Two-wing or a Four-wing, and your personality as a whole can best be understood by considering the traits of the Three as they uniquely blend with the traits of either the Two or the Four. In our teaching experience over the years, we have also encountered some individuals who seem to have *both* wings, while still others are so strongly influenced by their basic type that they show little of either wing.

There is disagreement among the various traditions of the Enneagram about whether individuals have one or two wings. Strictly speaking, everyone has two wings — in the restricted sense that both of the types adjacent to your basic type are operative in your personality since each person possesses the potentials of all nine types. However, this is not what is usually meant by "having two wings," and proponents of the so-called two-wing theory believe that both wings operate more or less equally in everyone's personality. (For example, they believe that a Three would have roughly equal amounts of his or her Two and Four wings.)

Observation of people leads us to conclude that while the two-wing theory applies to some individuals, most people have a *dominant wing*. In the vast majority of people, while the so-called second wing always remains operative to some degree, the dominant wing is far more important. (For example, Twos with a Three-wing are noticeably different from Twos with a One-wing, and while Twos with a Three-wing have a One-wing, it is not nearly as important as the Three-wing.) It is therefore clearer to refer simply to a type's "wing" as opposed to its "dominant wing," since the two terms represent the same concept.

One other observation about wings is worth mentioning. Many people in the latter half of their lives have reported the development of their so-called "second wing." And in individuals who have been pursuing psychological and/or spiritual work, we have seen evidence that this is true. We do not know, however, whether these students were merely seeing all of the positive potentials of the nine types unfolding in them as they matured — their second wing being one of the other seven types — or whether this was a specific development of the second wing type. The authors will continue to investigate this idea in our work with our students and colleagues.

It is, of course, necessary to identify your basic type before you can assess which wing you have. Besides indicating your basic type, the *Riso-Hudson Enneagram Type Indicator* (RHETI, version 2.5) may also indicate your wing. Even so, the best way to understand the influence of your wing is to read the full descriptions of your type and its wings in *Personality Types*. You can also read the descriptions of the two types adjacent to your basic type and decide which best applies to you.

The Levels of Development

There is an internal structure within each personality type. That structure is the continuum of behaviors, attitudes, defenses, and motivations formed by the nine Levels of Development that make up the personality type itself. This discovery (and the working out of all the traits that comprise each type) was made by Don Riso in 1977 and has been subsequently developed with Russ Hudson in the last ten years. They are the only Enneagram teachers to include this important factor in their treatment of the Enneagram. The Levels are an important contribution not only to the Enneagram but to ego psychology — and the personality types of the Enneagram cannot be adequately explained without them. The Levels account for differences between people of the same type as well as how people change both for better or worse. Thus, they can also help therapists and counselors pinpoint what is actually going on with clients and suggest solutions to the problems they are having.

The Levels of Development provide a framework for seeing how all of the different traits that comprise each type fit into a large whole; they are a way of conceptualizing the underlying "skeletal" structure of each type. Without the Levels, the types can seem to be an arbitrary collection of unrelated traits, with contradictory behaviors and attitudes often part of the picture. But by understanding the Levels for each type, one can see how all of the traits are interrelated — and how healthy traits can deteriorate into average traits and possibly into unhealthy ones. As pioneering consciousness philosopher Ken Wilber has noted, without the Levels, the Enneagram is reduced to a "horizontal" set of nine discrete categories. By including the Levels, however, a "vertical" dimension is added that not only reflects the complexity of human nature but goes far in explaining many different, important elements within personality.

Further, with the Levels, a *dynamic* element is introduced that reflects the changing nature of the personality patterns themselves. You have probably noticed that people change constantly — sometimes they are clearer, more free, grounded, and emotionally available, while at other times they are more anxious, resistant, reactive, emotionally volatile, and less free. Understanding the Levels makes it clear that when people change states within their personality, they are shifting within the spectrum of motivations, traits, and defenses that make up their personality type.

To understand an individual accurately, it is necessary to perceive where the person lies along the continuum of Levels of his or her type at a given time. In other words, one must assess whether a person is in his or her healthy, average, or unhealthy range of functioning. This is important because, for example, two people of the same personality type and wing will differ significantly if one is healthy and the other unhealthy. (In relationships and in the business world, understanding this distinction is crucial.)

The continuum is comprised of nine internal Levels of Development — briefly, there are three Levels in the healthy section, three Levels in the average section, and three Levels in the unhealthy section. It may help you to think of the continuum of Levels as a photographer's gray scale, with gradations from pure white to pure black with many shades of gray in between. On the continuum, the healthiest traits appear first, at the top, so to speak. As we move down the continuum in a spiral pattern, we progressively pass through each Level of Development, marking a distinct shift in the personality's deterioration to the pure black of psychological breakdown at the bottom. The continuum for each of the personality types can be seen in the following diagram.

	Level 1	The Level of Liberation
Healthy	Level 2	The Level of Psychological Capacity
	Level 3	The Level of Social Value
	Level 4	The Level of Imbalance/Social Role
Average	Level 5	The Level of Interpersonal Control
	Level 6	The Level of Overcompensation
	Level 7	The Level of Violation
Unhealthy	Level 8	The Level of Obsession and Compulsion
	Level 9	The Level of Pathological Destructiveness

The Continuum of the Levels of Development

At each Level, significant psychological shifts occur as indicated by the title we have given to it. For example, at Level 5, the Level of Interpersonal Control, the person is trying to manipulate himself and others to get his psychological needs met. This invariably creates interpersonal conflicts. By this Level, the person has also fully identified with the ego and does not see himself as anything more than that: the ego must therefore be increasingly defended and inflated for the person to feel safe and to keep his or her identity intact. If this activity does not satisfy the person, and anxiety increases, he or she may deteriorate to the next state, Level 6, the Level of Overcompensation, where behavior will become more intrusive and aggressive as the person continues to pursue his or her ego-agenda. Anxiety is increasing, and the person is increasingly disruptive and focused on getting his or her needs met, regardless of the impact on people around them.

One of the most profound ways of understanding the Levels is as *a measure of our capacity to be present.* The more we move *down* the Levels, the more identified we are with our ego and its increasingly negative and restrictive patterns. Our personality becomes more defensive, reactive, and automatic — and we consequently have less and less real freedom and less real consciousness. As we move down the Levels, we become caught in more compulsive, destructive actions that are ultimately self-defeating.

By contrast, the movement *up the Levels* toward health is simultaneous with being more present and awake in our minds, hearts, and bodies. As we become more present, we become less fixated in the defensive structures of our personality and are more attuned and open to ourselves and our environment. We see our personality objectively in action rather than "falling asleep" to our automatic personality patterns. There is therefore the possibility of "not doing" our personality and of gaining some real distance from the negative consequences of getting caught in it.

As we become more present, we see our personality more objectively, and the Levels become a constant guide to self-observation, a map that we can use to chart where we are in our psychospiritual development at any given time. As we move "up" the Levels, we discover that we are freer and less driven by compulsive, unconscious drives and therefore able to act more effectively in all areas of our lives, including in our relationships. When we are less identified with our personality, we find that we respond as needed to whatever life presents, actualizing the positive potentials in all nine types, bringing real peace, creativity, strength, joy, compassion, and other positive qualities to whatever we are doing. (For more, see *Personality Types*, 45–51, 421–26, 465–93; *Understanding the Enneagram*, 136–66; and *The Wisdom of the Enneagram*, 75–87.)

Directions of Integration (Security) and Disintegration (Stress)

As we have seen with the Levels of Development, the nine personality types of the Enneagram are not static categories: they reflect our change over time. Further, the sequence of the types and the arrangement of the inner lines of the symbol are not arbitrary. The inner lines of the Enneagram connect the types in a sequence that denotes what each type will do under different conditions. Two lines connect to each type. One line connects with another type that represents how the person behaves when he or she feels more secure and in control of a situation. This is called the Direction of Integration or the Security Point. The other line goes to another type that represents how the person is likely to act out under increased stress and pressure — when he or she feels *not* in control of the situation. This second line is called the Direction of Stress or Disintegration. In other words, different situations will evoke different kinds of responses from your personality. You will respond or adapt in different directions, as indicated by the lines of the Enneagram *from your basic type.* Again, we see the flexibility and dynamism of the Enneagram.

The *Direction of Stress* or *Disintegration* for each type is indicated by the sequence of numbers 1–4–2–8–5–7–1 and 9–6–3–9. This means that under stress, an average to unhealthy One will behave like an average to unhealthy Four; an average to unhealthy Four will act out stress like an average to unhealthy Two; an average to unhealthy Two will act out under stress like an Eight; an Eight will act out under stress like a Five; a Five will act out like a Seven; and a Seven will act out like a One. (An easy way to remember the sequence is to realize that 1–4 or 14 doubles to 28, and that doubles to 57 — or almost so. Thus, 1–4–2–8–5–7 — and the sequence returns to 1 and begins again.)

Likewise, on the equilateral triangle, the sequence is 9–6–3–9: a Nine under long-term stress will act out like a Six; a Six under stress will act out like a Three; and a Three under stress will act out like a Nine. (You can remember this sequence if you think of the numerical values diminishing as the types become more stressed and reactive. For a longer explanation and examples, see *Personality Types*, 47–52, 413–8.) You can see how this works by following the direction of the arrows on the following Enneagram.

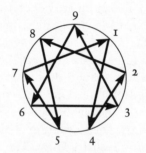

The Direction of Disintegration
1-4-2-8-5-7-1
9-6-3-9

The *Direction of Integration* or *Security* is indicated for each type by the *reverse* of the sequences for Disintegration. Each type moves toward integration in a direction that is the opposite of its stress direction. Thus, the sequence for the Direction of Integration or Security is 1–7–5–8–2–4–1: an integrating One goes to Seven; an integrating Seven goes to Five; an integrating Five goes to Eight; an integrating Eight goes to Two; an integrating Two goes to Four; and an integrating Four goes to One. On the equilateral triangle, the sequence is 9–3–6–9: an integrating Nine will go to Three; an integrating Three will go to Six; and an integrating Six will go to Nine. You can see how this works by following the direction of the arrows on the following Enneagram.

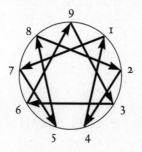

The Direction of Integration
1-7-5-8-2-4-1
9-3-6-9

It is not necessary to have separate Enneagrams for the Direction of Integration and the Direction of Disintegration. Both directions can be shown on one Enneagram by eliminating the arrows and connecting the proper points with plain lines.

The Direction of Integration   **The Direction of Stress**
1-7-5-8-2-4-1   1-4-2-8-5-7-1
9-3-6-9   9-6-3-9

No matter what personality type you are, the types in *both* your Direction of Integration and your Direction of Stress or Disintegration are important influences. To obtain a complete picture of yourself (or of someone else), you must take into consideration the basic type and wing as well as the two types in the Directions of Integration and Disintegration. The factors represented by those *four* types blend into your total personality and provide the framework for understanding the influences operating in you. For example, no one is simply a personality type Two. A Two has either a One-wing or a Three-wing, and the Two's Direction of Stress (Eight) and its Direction of Security or Integration (Four) also play important parts in his or her overall personality.

Ultimately, the goal is for each of us to "move around" the Enneagram, integrating what each type symbolizes and acquiring the healthy potentials of *all the types*. The ideal is to become a balanced, fully functioning person who can draw on the power (or from the Latin, *virtus*) of each as needed. Each of the types of the Enneagram symbolizes different important aspects of what we need to achieve this end. (See Chapter 15 on the Functions.) The personality type we begin life with is therefore less important ultimately than how well (or badly) we use our type as the beginning point for our self-development and self-realization.

The Three Instincts

The Three Instincts (often erroneously called "the subtypes") are a third set of distinctions that are extremely important for understanding personality. A major aspect of human nature lies in our instinctual "hard wiring" as biological beings. We each are endowed with specific instinctual intelligences that are necessary for our survival as individuals and as a species. We each have a *self-preservation instinct* (for preserving the body and its life and functioning), a *sexual instinct* (for extending ourselves in the environment and through the generations), and a *social instinct* (for getting along with others and forming secure social bonds).

These instinctual drives profoundly influence our personalities, and, at the same time, our personalities largely determine how each person *prioritizes* these instinctual needs. Thus, while every human being has all three of these instincts operating in him or her, our personality causes us to be more concerned with one of these instincts than the other two. We call this instinct our *dominant* instinct. This tends to be our first priority — the area of life we attend to first. But when we are more caught up in the defenses of our personality — further down the Levels of Development — our personality mostly *interferes* with our dominant instinct.

Further, our Enneagram type flavors the way in which we approach our dominant instinctual need. Combining our Enneagram type with our dominant instinct yields a much more specific portrait of the workings of our personality. When we apply the distinctions of these three instincts to the nine Enneagram types, they create twenty-seven unique combinations of type and dominant instinct that account for differences and variability within the types. We call these combinations the Instinctual Variants. (See the individual types in this book and in *The Wisdom of the Enneagram* for more information about the Instinctual Variants.)

The following sections provide brief descriptions of the three instincts.

Self-Preservation (a.k.a. "Nesting") Instinct

People who have this as their dominant instinct are preoccupied with the safety, comfort, health, energy, and well-being of the physical body. In a word, they are concerned with having enough *resources* to meet life's demands. Identification with the body is a fundamental focus for all humans, and we need our body to function well in order to be alive and active in the world. Most people in contemporary cultures are not faced with life or death "survival" in the strictest sense; thus, Self-Preservation (or Self-Pres) types tend to be concerned with food, money, housing, medical matters, and physical comfort. Moreover, those primarily focused on self-preservation, by extension, are usually interested in maintaining these resources *for others* as well. Their focus of attention naturally goes toward things related to these areas, such as clothes, temperature, shopping, decorating, and the like, particularly if they are not satisfied in these areas or have a feeling of deprivation due to their childhoods. Self-Pres types tend to be more grounded, practical, serious, and introverted than the other two instinctual types. They might have active social lives and a satisfying intimate relationship, but if they feel that their self-preservation needs are not being met, they still tend not to be happy or at ease. In their primary relationships, these people are "nesters" — they seek domestic tranquility and security with a stable, reliable partner.

Sexual (a.k.a. "Intimate") Instinct

Many people initially identify themselves as this type because they have learned that the sexual types are interested in "one-on-one relationships." But all three instinctual types are interested in one-on-one relationships for different reasons, so this does not distinguish them. The key element in sexual types is an intense drive for intimacy and a constant awareness of the "chemistry" between themselves and others. Sexual types are immediately aware of the attraction, or lack thereof, between themselves and other people. Further, while the basis of this instinct is related to sexuality, it is not necessarily about engaging in the sexual act. There are many people we are excited to be around for reasons of personal chemistry that we have no intention of "getting involved with." Nonetheless, we might be aware that we feel stimulated in certain people's company and less so in others. People of the sexual instinct are constantly moving toward that sense of intense stimulation and intimacy in their relationships and in their activities. They are the most "energized" of the three instinctual types, tending to be more aggressive, competitive, charged, and emotionally intense than the Self-Pres or Social types. Sexual types need to have deep *intimacy* in their primary relationships, or else they remain unsatisfied. They enjoy being intensely involved — even merged — with others and can become disenchanted with partners who are unable to meet their need for intense energetic union. Losing yourself in a "fusion of being" is the ideal here, and Sexual types are always looking for this state with others and with stimulating objects in their world.

Social (a.k.a. "Adaptive") Instinct

Just as many people tend to misidentify themselves as Sexual types because they want one-on-one relationships, many people fail to recognize themselves as Social types because they get the (false) idea that this means always being involved in groups, meetings, and parties. If Self-Pres types are interested in adjusting the environment to make themselves more secure and comfortable, Social types *adapt themselves to serve the needs of the social situation* they find themselves in. Thus, Social types are highly aware of other people, whether they are in intimate situations or in groups. They are also aware of how their actions and attitudes affect those around them. Moreover, where Sexual types seek intimacy, Social types seek *personal connection:* they want to stay in long-term contact with people and to be involved in their world. Social types are the most concerned with doing things that will have some impact on their community or even broader domains. They tend to be warmer, more open, engaging, and socially responsible than the other two types. In their primary relationships, they seek partners with whom they can share social activities, wanting their intimates to get involved in projects and events with them. Paradoxically, they actually tend to avoid long periods of exclusive intimacy and quiet solitude, seeing both as potentially limiting. Social types lose their sense of identity and meaning when they are not involved with others in activities that transcend their individual interests.

Typing Yourself and Others

Once you have used the *Riso-Hudson Enneagram Type Indicator* to discover your dominant type, you may be curious about the personality types of others. Since you will usually not be able to administer the RHETI to business associates or to strangers, you might wonder how you can become more skilled at discovering what type someone else is. By studying the descriptions in *Personality Types, Understanding the Enneagram,* and *The Wisdom of the Enneagram,* you will become more adept at typing people. As you do so, however, you might keep several points in mind.

You may be able to figure out the types of a few close friends rather quickly, or you may find it difficult to categorize people and not know where to begin. Either state is normal. It is not always apparent what type someone is, and it takes time and study to sharpen your skills. Remember that you are like a beginning medical student who is learning to diagnose a wide variety of conditions, some healthy and some unhealthy. It takes practice to learn to identify the various "symptoms" of each type and to see larger "syndromes."

Despite the subtleties and complexities involved, there is really no secret about typing people. You must learn which traits go with each type and observe how people manifest those traits. This is a subtle undertaking because there are many contradictions and quirks to each personality type. Different types can sometimes seem similar, particularly if their motivations are not taken into account. This is why it is not sufficient to focus on a single trait in isolation and make a diagnosis based on it alone. It is necessary to see each type as a whole — its overall style, approach to life, and especially its underlying motivations — before you can determine someone's type reliably. Many elements must come together before you can be sure that you have typed someone accurately.

Moreover, when we diagnose others, we are always on thinner ice than when we use the Enneagram to deepen our own self-knowledge. It is, of course, more appropriate to apply this material to ourselves than to type others while we avoid looking at our own lives. Nevertheless, it is unrealistic to think that anything as interesting (or as insightful) as the Enneagram will not be used for better understanding others. In fact, we categorize people all the time. No one approaches others without some set of mental categories. We automatically perceive people either as male or female, black or white, attractive or unattractive, good or bad, friend or enemy, and so forth. It is not only honest to be aware of this, it is useful to develop more accurate and appropriate categories for everyone, including ourselves.

Although the Enneagram is probably the most open-ended and dynamic of typologies, this does not imply that the Enneagram can say all there is to say about human beings. Individuals are understandable only up to a certain point, beyond which they remain mysterious and unpredictable. Thus, while there can be no simple explanations for people as individuals, it is still possible to say something true about them. In the last analysis, the Enneagram helps us to do that — and only that. The Enneagram is useful because it indicates with startling clarity certain constellations of meaning about something that is essentially beyond definition: the mystery of who we are.

6. Type One: The Reformer

The Rational, Idealistic Type: Principled, Purposeful, Self-Controlled, and Perfectionistic

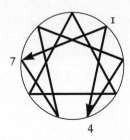

Generally, Ones are conscientious, sensible, responsible, idealistic, ethical, serious, self-disciplined, orderly, and feel personally obligated to improve themselves and their world.

Ones get into conflicts by being opinionated, impatient, irritable, rigid, perfectionistic, critical (and self-critical), sarcastic, and judgmental.

At their best, Ones are tolerant, accepting, discerning, wise, humane, prudent, principled, fair, and able to delay rewards for a higher good.

Recognizing Ones

Type One exemplifies the desire to be good, to live up to the highest ethical standards, and to effect positive changes in the world. While a number of types care about achieving goals, Ones are particularly aware of *how* they achieve their goals. Were they honorable? Did they use their resources wisely? Were they fair and truthful? Ones are people of high standards, and they expect themselves and others to live by those standards as much as possible. They tend to see things in terms of long-range objectives, and they can be aware of how current actions might affect future situations. For example, Ones are often in the forefront of battles to improve environmental standards or to make people aware of healthier lifestyle choices.

Most Ones report feeling a powerful *sense of mission*, a deep feeling of purpose that they remember from their early childhood. They sense that they are here for a reason, and, unlike some other types, they have a fairly clear idea of what that reason is. This sense of mission impels Ones to rise to their highest standards, to make personal sacrifices, and to evaluate themselves regularly to see if they are falling short of their ideals. They feel that they must live a balanced, sensible life in order to have the clarity and inner resources necessary to fulfill their purpose.

Ones also have deep convictions about right and wrong, what is just and unjust. They are often dedicated to reform and social causes because they feel personally obligated to improve the world and leave it a better place. They put themselves on the line for their values and ethical convictions — even if it means risking their jobs, their fortunes, or their very lives. Ones are convinced that there are indeed some truths — and some values — that are worth both living and dying for. To accomplish their missions, Ones maintain self-discipline and do their best to practice "moderation in all things."

While Ones focus their attention on serious life issues, their high standards can also be directed to less significant matters — although they may *seem* equally important to Ones at the time. They can become extremely upset, for instance, if their spouse or one of their children fails to clean up after themselves adequately after using the bathroom sink. Ones are nothing if not thorough and well organized. Some Ones express this as an extraordinary concern with "neatness," the kind of people whose socks and underwear are folded neatly, whose file folders are labeled and filed alphabetically, and whose pencils are all sharpened. Other Ones focus their perfectionism in other areas, such as punctuality, ethical standards, political or religious ideals, office protocols, or uncovering misdeeds and untruths.

While Ones tend to see themselves as people of logic and reason, they are often driven by strong feelings and impulses — usually experienced as personal convictions. Because they so strongly feel that they must accomplish their life mission, they conclude that they must be serious and determined and must not waste time. They can become very strict with themselves, feeling they must always be working toward their ideals, "making progress," and pointing out how things could be improved. They are extremely conscientious about how they use their time and resources. Under pressure, time becomes a major interpersonal issue for Ones — they insist that they and others be punctual, efficient, and particular about details. They make lists, organize things, and prioritize their activities constantly. Their sense of obligation, however, can make them feel heavier and more burdened. Consequently, they begin to be afraid of making a mistake because they want everything to be consistent with their strict standards. At such times, others can perceive them as overly rigid and perfectionistic.

In brief, Ones want to be right, to strive higher and improve everything, to be consistent with their ideals, to justify themselves, and to be beyond criticism so as not to be condemned by anyone. **Ones do not want** to be proven wrong, to make mistakes, to allow sloppiness, to be with people they perceive as lazy or not serious, to be in chaos or in situations that seem out of control, or to be embarrassed by emotional display.

Their Hidden Side

Ones appear well balanced and sure of themselves, but they can suffer from extreme self-criticism, feeling that they are never able to measure up to their Olympian standards. Similarly, they can feel lonely and alienated from others, seeing themselves as the only responsible adult around. At such times they feel burdened by their responsibilities and by the sense that others will not do as thorough a job as they will. If these feelings intensify, Ones can become harsh with themselves and others and can fall prey to hidden depression. They may attempt to maintain an outer attitude of self-control and reserve while inwardly feeling anguished and alienated. As they become more isolated, their self-criticism can become more cruel and irrational. Few casual observers would suspect how much they are suffering from the relentless attacks of their Inner Critic (superego).

Relationship Issues

Ones take their relationships and all of their responsibilities in relationships very seriously. They are firmly committed to the people whom they love, and they are willing to make great personal sacrifices for the well-being of their intimates. As with other areas of life, Ones are idealistic and hold high standards for their relationships — it is important to them to have a partnership that is based on shared values and beliefs. When Ones get more stuck in their fixation, the following areas can create problems:

- Holding the partner to strict standards that the partner does not wholeheartedly share.
- Having difficulty finding a partner because of unrealistic standards — finding that no one "measures up."
- Becoming moody, depressed, and uncommunicative because of repressed anger.
- Not allowing enough "play time" in the relationship — feeling that all spare time must be used for serious purposes (yard work, checking finances, reading "educational" or "meaningful" books, attending meetings or lectures, discussing political issues, etc.).
- Having issues with criticism: fearing criticism from a partner and also becoming critical of the partner — nitpicking, scolding, and correcting.

The Passion: Anger or Resentment

Feelings of obligation and of having higher standards than those around them leave Ones in a state of constant irritation with themselves, others, and the world. Nothing ever quite attains the ideal; nothing comes up to their exacting standards, leaving them feeling disappointed, frustrated, and resentful. But because such feelings conflict with their self-image of being rational and in control of themselves, they attempt to suppress their anger, unwittingly perpetuating it in the process. They become very inhibited, feeling that they must constantly hold their angry feelings and impulses in check. Ones may also hold their anger in their bodies, and they can become extremely tense and rigid with the effort to control themselves.

At Their Best

Healthy Ones are guided by their consciences and concerned with maintaining ethical standards, but they are also flexible and gentle about applying their principles — both with themselves and with others. They are truthful and reasonable — the kind of person others turn to for direction and clear feedback. They have a strong sense of morality, but they temper this with a deep love and respect for the dignity of their fellow human beings. They strive to be impartial, fair, and objective, and they are willing to sublimate their desires and immediate gratification for "the greater good," or a higher principle.

Healthy Ones are motivated to "do the right thing" themselves and are not necessarily trying to fix anyone else. Even so, their personal integrity allows them to teach others by example. They can be quite eloquent and effective at conveying the truth and wisdom of their perspective. They stand for quality and desire excellence in all things. Their commitment to the highest principles can be profoundly moving to others, reminding others of the values they most deeply cherish.

At their best, high-functioning Ones embody true wisdom, especially in being able to discern appropriate and compassionate action. They radiate nobility and inspire others to remember to live according to the highest values. At the same time, they are gentle and humane: average Ones often feel disappointed with their fellow human beings, but healthy Ones feel a profound connection and kinship with everyone they encounter, giving them an abiding patience and affection for all humanity.

Personality Dynamics and Variations

Under Stress (One Goes to Average Four)

Ones begin to feel alienated and moody when they sense that others do not take them or their values seriously. They feel obligated to do the work they believe others will not do — or will not do *as well* — and they become more resentful. They feel misunderstood by their peers and often withdraw from others to sort out their feelings, much like average-to-unhealthy Fours. Similarly, Ones under prolonged stress can become disillusioned with themselves and their lot in life. Over time, they can become depressed and isolated, often turning to self-indulgent behavior in an attempt to feel better. They allow themselves various "escape hatches" — indulgences that go against their expressed values in some way. For instance, a One who is scrupulously observing rigorous health regimens and diets might start treating herself to ice cream sodas or chocolate bars. Guilt usually follows, leaving her more depressed and critical of herself.

Security (One Goes to Average Seven)

Ones become more playful and uninhibited in the company of people with whom they feel safe. It is as though a secure environment gives Ones permission to let their "silly side" out, along with the ability to express a more complete range of their emotions. They can be funny, talkative, tell jokes and long stories, and can lead others into adventures of various kinds. They can also be boldly outspoken, impulsive, and "naughty" when they feel they can get away with it. They can allow some of their needs to surface and become demanding, selfish, and greedy after the manner of a low-average Seven. Under stress, they may inadvertently look for distractions and begin to scatter their focus and their energies, as if to prevent becoming overwhelmed by the pressures they feel both from the obligations they have taken on and from their superego.

Integration (One Goes to Healthy Seven)

As Ones work through the basic issues of their type, they become less strict with themselves and begin to enjoy a greater freedom, lightness, and spontaneity, like healthy Sevens. Instead of feeling that everything is a personal obligation, they begin to experience choice, freedom, abundance, and joy. Whatever they do will be good and worthwhile, and they begin to live by the maxim, "Whatever is worth doing is worth doing badly." They let themselves off the hook of their strident superegos and begin to recognize what they want rather than what they "must" or "should" do. Integrating Ones can more easily access their curiosity and intelligence — their minds are open to many new possibilities. Their lighter approach helps other people hear their views and allows Ones to feel much closer to their fellow human beings. Rather than feeling resentful and obligated, they are filled with gratitude and a deep acceptance of themselves and others.

The Instincts In Brief

Self-Preservation Ones: Self-Control (Ichazo's "Anxiety")

Self-Preservation Ones focus their resentment and perfectionism in areas of health, self-management, and homemaking. They are not necessarily worked up about the plight of refugees in the Third World but may have very firm convictions about proper diet and exercise or the best way to maintain one's household or family budget. Self-Pres Ones like to be organized, to have their life structured, and their possessions put in their proper place. They are neat, punctual, and fastidious — sometimes to a fault. They believe that controlling the "dirt" and chaos in their lives will enhance their well-being, even their survival. It seems to them that a well-ordered life is the best hedge against chaos and danger, and they are concerned that any mistakes on their part could have dire consequences. Thus, they tend to be careful and meticulous in the planning of their lives. Many Self-Pres Ones also take an active interest in preventative health matters: vitamins, cleansing diets and fasts, exercise routines, alternative medicine, and cutting-edge medical knowledge.

Sexual Ones: Shared Standards (Ichazo's "Jealousy")

Sexual Ones focus their perfectionism on their intimate relationships, holding an ideal image of what a relationship should be like and measuring their intimates against this standard. For this reason, many Sexual Ones have difficulty finding a life partner that meets their criteria — there is always some characteristic in the potential mate that falls short of their expectations. They may also harbor expectations of creating a perfect family, but this must begin with finding a mate who understands and shares their passion for their mission. When Sexual Ones find a partner who they believe shares their values, they become extremely excited and highly protective of their relationship. They may also idealize the partner, constantly striving to feel worthy of the other's love. Nonetheless, anxieties about the partner's losing the shared values may cause Sexual Ones to become critical of the other. They want to remind the partner of the high standards that they both live by but they can create problems in the relationship by trying to keep the other "on track." Nonetheless, they are passionate about their intimates and devoted to keeping their relationships moving toward higher ground.

Social Ones: The Crusader (Ichazo's "Inadaptability")

Social Ones focus their perfectionism in the social realm; thus, they are interested in local and world affairs. What is going on with the school district? Has that new environmental legislation been passed? Why doesn't anyone care about the enormous problem of world hunger? Social Ones take these issues personally, and they devote their time and energy to bringing people's attention to social ills. In other words, they do not want merely to talk about problems, they want to get involved and take action. While they may work tirelessly for the causes that they care about, Social Ones may have trouble developing a personal life. They are not particularly interested in social ease, for themselves or for others; rather, they are concerned with finding the "right way" for people to conduct themselves with one another. When they are more identified with this attitude, they may feel that others do not know what is best for them. With regard to themselves, Social Ones feel that personal needs can be addressed only after more pressing social problems have been faced. This zeal can be hard on their families and intimates, but people are often amazed by the strength of the Social One's convictions and are grateful for the good work that they contribute to the community.

Ones grow by recognizing that others take things seriously, too, but that their approach to problems or tasks is often different. As they become more healthy and grounded, they become not only respectful of others' views but also curious about them. They understand that their own wisdom can only be enriched by taking other perspectives into account. Ones also grow by *playing* — by finding areas of their lives that are lighter, freer, and that offer opportunities for spontaneous creativity. Most Ones have a great sense of humor, and the more they allow themselves to entertain and enjoy others, the better for everyone involved. Basically, Ones grow to the extent that they can accept reality with all of its apparent contradictions and "imperfections." This, of course, especially applies to themselves. By *accepting what is,* and working with reality rather than judging it, they become transcendentally realistic, knowing the best action to take in each moment.

See also *Personality Types,* 376–409; *Understanding the Enneagram,* 63–65, 126–33, and 352–54; and *The Wisdom of the Enneagram,* 97–124.

7. Type Two: The Helper

The Caring, Interpersonal Type:
Demonstrative, Generous, People-Pleasing,
and Possessive

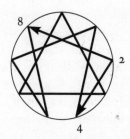

Generally, Twos are caring, empathetic, warm, thoughtful, appreciative, generous, other-oriented, tactile, affectionate, well intentioned, and demonstrative.

Twos get into conflicts by being people-pleasing, flattering, ingratiating, clingy, worried, possessive, insincere, seductive, self-important, and self-deceptive.

At their best, Twos are encouraging, loving, self-nurturing, constant, joyous, humble, forgiving, gracious, and compassionate.

Recognizing Twos

Type Two exemplifies the desire to feel loved, to connect with others in a heartfelt way, and to be a source of benevolence and love in our world. Twos are easily the most people-oriented of the Enneagram types. They focus on relationship and feel best about themselves when they are meaningfully engaged with others. They want to share the good in their lives and genuinely enjoy supporting others with their attention and care. Insofar as they can, Twos make good things happen for people. They will stay up late to take care of children or older folks, drive across town to bring food, or see to it that others get medical treatment. When there is practical work to be done for others, healthy Twos will be there, throwing themselves into the effort heart and soul.

Twos are genuinely interested in other people and in the details of their lives. They remember to send birthday and holiday cards long after their friends have moved away. They also remember your spouse's name and the names of your children and pets — plus who has which allergies and what their major was in college. Twos are the first in the kitchen after a party to help out with the cleanup. At the office, Twos have a bowl of candy or a tin of cookies at their desk — not for themselves, but for anyone who drops by to chat. They are constantly thinking of others, and they try to do nice things so that others will think well of them.

Twos get into difficulty, however, when they begin to attend to others' needs without adequately dealing with their own. They can get into denial about the extent of their own needs while insisting that their only concern is taking care of others. At such times, Twos may develop "boundary problems." They disregard their own boundaries, doing things for others that take them away from what they need to do for themselves, *and* they disregard the boundaries of others, doing things for others that they do not necessarily want done. When others feel crowded by the Twos' efforts to help, and try to set boundaries with them, Twos can feel hurt and insecure about the relationship and feel rejected.

When Twos doubt that others want them, they redouble their efforts to win people over. They get caught up with "people pleasing" and ingratiating themselves with others, looking for things to do and say that will make people like them. "Relating" with people becomes a full-time job: they are constantly making new friends while maintaining a network of old friends. Talking about "the relationship" with people becomes a habit, as Twos continually seek reassurance that their friendships and love-lives are secure and on track.

They also begin to seek ways to make themselves more interesting and useful to others. Thus, they may pursue such interests as massage, psychic readings, energetic healing, nutrition, and other ways of being of service as a way of making people feel good about themselves — *and about having the Two in their life*. They want to have a unique place in others' lives and to know privileged information about others that no one else knows. They want others to regard them as their "best friend," to seek them out for personal advice, and to share special secrets and intimacies. They may begin to wear themselves out for others, giving unwanted advice and assistance, and becoming "martyrs" to get attention and affection. When Twos go too far with this kind of behavior, however, it ironically has the opposite effect on people — driving them away rather than creating stronger relationships.

In brief, Twos want to feel loved, to have intimacy, to express their feelings for others, to be needed and appreciated, to be close to valued friends and family, to "rescue" potential friends and partners, to get others to respond to them, and to get and hold on to the love they want. **Twos do not want** to be out of touch with loved ones, to be in impersonal settings, to be left out of social situations, or to be in situations where there is nothing for them to give.

Their Hidden Side

Although on the surface Twos appear to feel at ease with others and to be a source of emotional sustenance for the people in their lives, they also suffer from well-hidden feelings of rejection. Twos expect people to not want them around, and they often feel that they need to be extraordinarily kind and supportive to get people to accept and love them. They usually try to conceal the depths of their loneliness or hurt beneath an image of concern for others, focusing on others' needs to help them feel better. Sometimes it does, but, just as often, Twos may feel that others are not appreciating them for their efforts, thus rekindling their feelings of rejection. Then they may become touchy or even openly angry, revealing the extent of the disappointment they are hiding.

Relationship Issues

Twos are the Enneagram type most focused on relationships: people are where Twos focus their energies. They are generous with their time and attention and really want their loved ones to be happy and well-cared for. Problems develop, however, when Twos go overboard with their efforts to be close to their loved ones, often in the following areas:

- Trying too hard to please the other — selling themselves out for affection and appreciation.
- Hovering around and not giving the other adequate space (usually caused by fears of imminent abandonment).
- Expecting "mind reading" from the partner and being disappointed when he or she fails to anticipate the Two's desires or needs.
- Becoming possessive of the partner and jealous of him or her spending time with others.
- Not acknowledging personal hurts, needs, and anger until they become damaging to the relationship.

The Passion: Pride

Twos believe that they will be loved only if they are completely available to attend to the needs of others. To the extent that they succumb to this belief, they fear that others will reject them if they have needs or emotional hurts of their own. When Twos find themselves unable to acknowledge the extent of their emotional needs and desires, they fall into the passion of pride. From this position, they feel duty-bound to care for others while denying that they have any significant problems themselves. But of course, under the surface, Twos really *do* have many problems and longings. Unfortunately, the more Twos deny their real emotional condition, the more they tend to express themselves to others with covert aggression, ulterior motives, and hidden neediness. This often leads to behaviors that unintentionally drive other people away.

At Their Best

Healthy Twos are sincere and warm-hearted, with immense good will and enormous generosity of spirit. They have an extraordinary ability to feel the feelings and needs of others. Because they are so empathetic, healthy Twos know others' sorrows, and this motivates them to go out of their way to help and support people, especially in times of need. They put a charitable interpretation on the behavior of others, emphasizing the good in people whenever they find it. But healthy Twos are able to maintain this generous approach to life because they are acknowledging their own needs and, more importantly, addressing them.

Healthy Twos do not wait for a loving response from people in order to feel lovable. They recognize their true strengths and limitations and accept them — extending the support and love to themselves that they would easily offer to someone else. Thus, they are also able to accept others for who *they* are and relate to them on their own level, whether the person is the president of a corporation, the mailman, or a delivery boy. Twos see the dignity and the humanity of people and respond to that. They also foster independence in others, nurturing self-confidence, strength, and new skills so that people can grow on their own. They really want everyone to thrive and do not want anyone to be dependent on them, physically or psychologically. They are sincerely encouraging and extremely appreciative of the talents and strengths they find everywhere. Healthy Twos let people know the good they see in them, a quality that is particularly helpful to those who may not see much good in themselves.

Personality Dynamics and Variations

Under Stress (Two Goes to Average Eight)

If Twos feel that their overtures of friendliness and expressions of self-sacrifice are continually thwarted or ignored, they may reach a point of stress in which they begin to express their anger openly in the manner of average-to-unhealthy Eights. Their resentment at having been rejected by others (in perhaps subtle ways) reaches the boiling point, and they simply cannot maintain their "loving attitude" any longer. Feeling that others are taking them for granted makes the average Two suddenly act out in an average Eight manner, becoming egocentric, controlling, and dominating, telling people what to do and when to do it. This kind of behavior puts Twos in the center of things and virtually forces others to pay attention to them. Bossing people around and being somewhat confrontational can be surprisingly out of character for the Two. Under greater stress, it can result in outbursts of temper, aggressive confrontation, and threats of withdrawing support.

Security (Two Goes to Average Four)

With trusted others, or in situations in which Twos feel sure of themselves and their ability to be honest about their feelings, they may risk expressing their neediness and darker impulses. Rather than keep up the image of being selfless and above feeling wounded by the ingratitude of others, they can become moody, self-absorbed, and temperamental, revealing to intimates the true depth and extent of their emotional needs, self-doubts, and disappointments — particularly with others. At such times, they can be extremely touchy — easily hurt by statements that others would see as harmless or even positive. They may also become more self-indulgent, giving themselves "goodies" that are *not* very good for them as a way of compensating for all of the sacrifices they feel they have been making for others.

Integration (Two Goes to Healthy Four)

Integrating Twos become aware of how much they have denied their needs and their darker feelings — and how much they have deceived themselves about their motives. At Four, they begin to accept themselves more completely, not rejecting any aspect of themselves they find. Even their destructive feelings toward others can be held compassionately. They are more honest with themselves (after the manner of a healthy Four) and discover humor and humanity in whatever feelings and impulses they have. This gives Twos the ability to see themselves objectively and without shame — and with love and balance. They are also able to support others from the fullness of who they really are and to have greater intimacy with them, because integrating Twos are more intimate with themselves. Gradually and naturally, they become more authentic, expressive, sensitive, and creative in ways that are enriching to themselves and others.

The Instincts in Brief

Self-Preservation Twos: Entitlement (Ichazo's "Me First")

Twos typically deal with their own self-preservation needs by first taking care of *others'* self-preservation needs. They feel that they will win others' love by providing them with nurturing and caretaking. They derive a great deal of satisfaction from feelings of service to others or to causes. They are able to anticipate people's needs and then try to fulfill them. ("You poor thing, you look hungry.") Of course, after taking care of others for a while, Self-Pres Twos begin to expect that others will reciprocate and take care of *their* needs. But because they are Twos, they feel that they cannot ask directly for what they need. They must drop hints and continue to take care of the other person with the hope that he or she will eventually respond with care for the Two. Over time, this gives Self-Pres Twos a feeling of entitlement. ("After all I've done for them, I deserve this treat.") The problem is that Self-Pres Twos feel ashamed of having physical needs. Thus, when others fail to reciprocate in the way that Twos hope, they may privately overindulge in self-preservation "goodies" — comfort foods, sweets, drink, and prescription medicines are frequent choices. They keep hidden stashes of their favorite indulgences as a way of compensating for feelings of loneliness and rejection. Unfortunately, the rewards that Self-Pres Twos give themselves often endanger their health and well being, which, ironically, undermines their ability to help others.

Sexual Twos: Craving Intimacy (Ichazo's "Aggression")

Sexual Twos feel that they will feel loved by attaining complete, profound intimacy with someone. Thus they are driven to be as close to their loved ones as possible. They attempt to win a place with people by focusing intensely on the other's needs, hopes, and interests. They enjoy the process of learning about potential partners and make it their business to become acquainted with the other's world. It is as if the Sexual Two were seeking to get "in synch" with the other in as many different ways as possible. Similarly, the Sexual Two will enjoy finding out what the other likes, whether it is a favorite food, cologne, style of music, or favorite place for vacationing. Needless to say, Sexual Twos will then do their best to provide these things for their intimates. Moreover, most people love to be the center of attention, and Sexual Twos know this, lavishing the other with attention, affection, and praise. In this sense, they are seductive — getting others interested in spending time with them by making the other their object of adoration. Sexual Twos also like to touch and be touched by the people they are drawn to, often initiating physical contact in a relationship — even in a friendship. When less balanced, Sexual Twos can become obsessed with a lover and can have great difficulty letting go of a relationship.

Social Twos: Everybody's Friend (Ichazo's "Ambition")

Social Twos feel loved by having an important place in the lives of their friends, family, and colleagues. They fear being left out of social events and gatherings, so they try to make themselves indispensable to whatever groups they are involved with. They often become advisors, mentors, matchmakers, and social-event coordinators for many people in their lives. They enjoy introducing people to one another and generally act as the "social hub" of whatever they are involved with. They derive great satisfaction from giving advice to trusted friends and often initiate new relationships by offering some kind of service or counsel. Social Twos have a subtle "radar" for people in need of a sympathetic audience and may appear with a smile and some kind words. They especially like to give counsel to people they see as important. While the pride of Twos does not allow them to have social ambitions of success and fame for themselves, they often achieve these things indirectly by becoming "the power behind the throne." Thus, they are able to rise socially by attaching themselves as advisors and primary supports to someone who is successful in some way. Social Twos tend to be outgoing and high-spirited, often resembling Sevens, and to get energy from their interactions with their friends. Indeed, Social Twos think of all of their colleagues and acquaintances as friends and their friends as family. They usually know the names of all of the local shopkeepers, the mailman, the waiters and bartenders at their favorite restaurants and bars, and so forth. When less balanced, Social Twos can scatter themselves in a large number of social commitments — trying to serve many people, but often causing primary relationships to suffer.

Twos grow by recognizing that caring for themselves and caring for others is not an either/or proposition. They can care for others effectively *only* when they are also caring for themselves and recognizing their own needs. Further, they come to understand that they can achieve real love and intimacy with others only if they truly have love and intimacy with themselves. For Twos, this means acknowledging their real feelings, even if they are not pretty or pleasant, and expressing their needs as they arise. It also entails recognizing when they are tired, lonely, or overextended. By paying attention to their own feelings and inner states, Twos naturally grow into finding a balance between taking care of themselves and their natural inclination to help others. Once grounded and clear about their motives, they are able to abide in the fullness of their hearts and to share this with others.

See also *Personality Types*, 59–94; *Understanding the Enneagram*, 40–42, 74–79, and 332–34; and *The Wisdom of the Enneagram*, 125–50.

8. Type Three: The Achiever

The Success-Oriented, Efficient Type: Adaptive, Excelling, Driven, and Image-Conscious

Generally, Threes are effective, competent, adaptable, goal-oriented, ambitious, organized, diplomatic, charming, into performance, and image-conscious.

Threes get into conflicts by being expedient, excessively driven, competitive, self-promoting, "appropriate" instead of sincere, boastful, and grandiose.

At their best, Threes are inner-directed, authentic, modest, admirable, well-adjusted, gracious, interested in others, and self-accepting.

Recognizing Threes

Type Three exemplifies our desire to be our best self, to develop all of our potentials, and to value ourselves and others. Threes are the "stars" of the personality types — people of tremendous drive, ambition, and belief in themselves. Threes want to excel, to be the best at whatever they do, and they are willing to put in the effort it takes to do so. Threes can be found at the gym, taking classes at night, putting in extra hours at work, learning how to coordinate their best colors when they dress — basically doing what it takes to shine. While Threes are energetic and ambitious, they are also diplomatic — they want to be liked and esteemed by others. They strive to be presentable and appropriate, not wanting to come across in ways that would be disapproved of. They know how to put their best foot forward and present themselves in a way that highlights their energy and confidence.

Threes are, above all, goal-oriented. They get a particular objective in their sights and then actively engage in activities that will bring them closer to whatever they seek. They pursue their dreams tirelessly and cannot understand why others are not similarly motivated. Thus, Threes also enjoy sharing self-development tips, explaining how to make money, lose weight, develop career skills, and so forth. They are hard workers, diligent and effective — and they like helping others to be that way too.

To achieve their goals, Threes learn to be highly adaptable. They are able to change course when necessary and may even do so several times, including a change of career, if that is what it takes. They may try different approaches to problems until they find a formula that seems the most effective. Similarly, Threes quickly adapt to different social settings, always wanting to be appropriate and to exemplify the values of whatever group they are in. While their adaptability can be an enormous asset, it can also be overdone, leaving Threes unsure of who they are or what their own deepest values are.

In all of their dealings, Threes value efficiency and effectiveness, and they are often prized by businesses for these values. They are extremely goal-driven and, once they are given a task to perform, will do their best to make sure that it is done as quickly and efficiently as possible. The problem is that Threes can be efficient to a fault — becoming accomplishment machines, brushing their real feelings and needs aside to "get the job done." This way of living can leave Threes feeling empty and emotionally isolated, despite the successes they may be having.

Problems arise because Threes learned in childhood that they are valuable only for their accomplishments and self-presentation. They believe that they will be loved only if they become extraordinary in some field of endeavor. Thus, the pressure to be outstanding in whatever they do is intense and draining. Even if they are not working at a career and are primarily keeping a home, they will strive to have the most outstanding home in their neighborhood, and to be "Super-Mom" or "Super-Dad." Threes find it difficult to stop or rest when they are caught up in their drive for success. They believe that to do so is to risk failure — and most Threes would rather die than fail and risk being humiliated. Their drive for success can also create conflicts with their personal or family life. Similarly, intimacy issues are not uncommon.

When Threes push themselves too hard and are unable to deliver everything that they would like to, they may resort to presenting successful images to others rather than letting people know their actual state or emotional condition. They attempt to convince others and themselves that they have no problems and that they are doing great, even though they may feel depressed or even burnt out. They believe that they can "fake it until they make it," but if Threes do not slow down to deal with their emotional problems, sooner or later, a crash is inevitable.

In brief, Threes want to feel valuable and worthwhile, to excel, to be affirmed, to be effective and efficient, to perform well, to be "the best," to have attention, to be admired, and to impress others. *Threes do not want* anything that looks like failure, to sit around "doing nothing," to be overshadowed by others, to look unprepared or awkward, to be average, to ask others for help or support, or to be caught in distortions of the truth.

Their Hidden Side

Beneath the surface, Threes have deep anxieties about their personal value. They feel that unless they maintain a certain position or image in life, they will be devalued, rejected, and tossed aside as worthless. Thus, they feel a constant inner pressure to "have it together," to not need much intimacy or personal support, and, above all, to constantly perform at maximum efficiency. Unless you knew a Three very well, you would never suspect the degree of emotional vulnerability and insecurity that they conceal beneath their smooth, efficient surface. The fact is that despite Threes' apparent social ease, there is great loneliness and a belief that they must not need help or support. As much as possible, Threes try to avoid their feelings of shame and isolation, but a large part of their growth entails allowing these feelings to arise and become integrated into their functioning self.

Relationship Issues

Threes often report that they feel confident in their ability to attract other people. They are usually charming and magnetic, and they know how to behave appropriately. Also, many Threes spend significant time and resources cultivating their personal presentation. They work at being in good physical condition and are often well-groomed. They want their partner to be proud of them and their accomplishments, so they often are drawn to people who they believe will appreciate them. The problem is that Threes fear that many parts of themselves may be less than outstanding or even unacceptable. Fears of potential rejection may prevent them from letting people get close to them. Significant relationship issues include the following:

- Presenting a favorable image that they later fear they will not be able to live up to.
- Fearing that people only want them for their looks or abilities.
- Not speaking up when they need help or support, then resenting the partner for not supporting them.
- Workaholism as a way of avoiding intimacy.
- Pre-emptively leaving relationships out of fear of rejection, or having serial relationships ("conquests") as a way of bolstering their self-image.
- Haranguing the partner for not reflecting well on them, for behaving in ways that do not support the Three's self-image.

The Passion: Deceit (Vanity)

Deceit here is primarily a kind of self-deception. Threes convince themselves that only their image and their performance are valuable. They subconsciously feel that their own natural inner qualities are inadequate or unacceptable, so they strive to become the sort of person that they believe others would look up to. They have an idea of the qualities, talents, and appearance that they need to have in order to be acceptable, and they work tirelessly to embody those qualities.

Thus, Threes convince themselves that they must always be outstanding, superb, and exceptional — the best at whatever they are focusing on. To be any less than this is to fail, to be worthless. This is like the child who gets straight A's but is then tormented by getting an A-minus or a B-plus, or the athlete who wins several gold medals but then feels like a failure for getting a silver or bronze. This kind of self-rejection and self-deception causes Threes a great deal of suffering. Once Threes lose themselves in these self-deceptions, truth becomes whatever works to keep their self-image going, and they are able to deceive others, often without any apparent remorse.

At Their Best

Healthy Threes are excellent communicators, motivators, and promoters, and they know how to present something in a way that's acceptable and attractive. In the workplace, they can be very effective at building morale and company spirit. They value excellence and accomplishment and truly enjoy helping others discover how to shine. Even when they are not "coaching" others, they often inspire people to become like them in some way.

Healthy Threes are able to do this because they believe in themselves and invest time and energy in developing their native talents. They value themselves, their lives, and the people they love, seeing life as an opportunity to offer what talents they have been given to the world. They are also "adaptable" in the best sense of the word. If they see that they are doing something incorrectly or that their methods are not reaping positive results, they are willing to learn another way and to change. Further, healthy Threes are not in a contest with anyone. They deeply enjoy working with others toward shared goals and do not need to outshine their peers.

Thus, healthy Threes may or may not have significant accomplishments, but others are impressed by their realness and their heartfelt sincerity. They model an honesty, simplicity, and authenticity that inspires people. They do not try to impress others or inflate their importance; rather, they see their limitations and appreciate their talents without taking themselves too seriously. At their best, they are also tender, touchingly genuine, and affectionate — they truly become "heroes" and "role models" who inspire others by their outstanding achievements, humility, and warmth.

Personality Dynamics and Variations

Under Stress (Three Goes to Average Nine)

When Threes drive themselves too hard, their stress can go beyond what they can normally cope with. When this occurs, they tend to go on "autopilot," attempting to just get through things without being bothered, in the manner of average Nines. Threes going to Nine become more passive and fall into routines. They lose their focus and involve themselves with busywork to at least give the appearance that they are getting things done. If stress continues, however, they may begin to shut down, becoming listless and depressed, losing interest in their projects, and withdrawing from people. They feel little energy or enthusiasm and simply want people to leave them alone and give them space. They can become stubborn and resistant to offers of help at these times, not wanting to hear that they have a problem.

Security (Three Goes to Average Six)

With most people, Threes make every effort to be diplomatic and well mannered. They do not want to say things that would be off-putting to people if they can avoid it. But when Threes feel that their relationships are secure, they can be more open about expressing their anxieties and frustrations. They may keep a "positive frame of mind" all day at work, only to come home and download their dissatisfaction onto their spouse or partner. ("I think my boss is going to go nuts on me when he finds out we still haven't got this report nailed down.") Feelings of self-doubt, dread, suspicion, and anger at others' incompetence can all surface in contrast to the Three's usual "can do" attitude.

Integration (Three Goes to Healthy Six)

As Threes let go of their fears of failure and worthlessness, they start to feel less competitive with others. They relax and find that they feel most valuable while working cooperatively with others toward shared goals and aspirations, like healthy Sixes. They learn to freely offer support and guidance to the people in their lives, but more importantly, they also learn to ask for support when they need it. Threes ordinarily put themselves under such pressure to accomplish their goals with little or no help that it comes as both a surprise and a relief to them that others are happy to help them in their endeavors. In short, Threes learn to trust others and to build lasting bonds with people. They become more selfless and courageous, embodying real qualities of leadership and self-sacrifice. By letting go of their need to outshine others, Threes become truly extraordinary human beings.

The Instincts in Brief

Self-Preservation Threes: The Workaholic (Ichazo's "Security")

Self-Preservation Threes feel their value is dependent on their ability to take care of basic security needs. They strive to be practical and to make sure that they and their family have more-than-adequate resources. For many Threes this means some kind of financial success. Thus, Self-Pres Threes work constantly to ensure they are building up a solid foundation. The problem is that they often find themselves unable to stop working. Because they believe their personal value is at stake, they cannot easily slow down or lighten their workload. To even take a weekend off could lead to financial failure — or so they believe. This lifestyle eventually takes its toll on their health and relationships. They may fit regular work-outs at the gym into their busy schedules in order to stay healthy but frequently neglect to rest and take quiet time. Others can find it difficult to make intimate contact with Self-Pres Threes once they are caught up in their drive for security and success.

Of the three instinctual variants of this type, the Self-Pres Three has the most difficulty contacting feelings. They tend to express affection through accomplishing things for their partner and by meeting practical expectations. But they may begin to see all of their relationships in terms of functional roles, transactions, task lists, and how well they and the people in their lives are fulfilling these roles. While this can be efficient up to a point, it often ends up creating distance between Self-Pres Threes and the people they care about.

Sexual Threes: The Catch (Ichazo's "Virility/Femininity")

Sexual Threes feel that their value comes from their desirability, so they do whatever they can to enhance their attractiveness to others. Many movie stars, models, and popular singers are Sexual Threes. They know how to project attractive qualities but also how to be a blank screen that others can project their desires onto. They often possess great charm and magnetism, yet they fear being dismissed by others for lacking some essential ingredient. As Sexual types, they want to have a strong intimate connection with someone, but because of the Three's image issues and underlying feelings of shame, they are often insecure about letting people know them too well. Thus, many Sexual Threes are able to gain attention and interest from others, but they fear that once they get someone's attention, they will be unable to keep it.

Sexual Threes want to be appreciated for their depth and intelligence too, but they fear that others are only interested in them for their attractiveness. Some Sexual Threes may go through periods of rebellion, downplaying their physical attributes for a while to see if people still like them and to find out more about themselves. Ultimately, this type grows by recognizing their own value directly — that is, without believing that it only exists reflected in the admiring eyes of others.

Social Threes: The Status Seeker (Ichazo's "Prestige")

Social Threes seek value by gaining social recognition — by having tangible signs of progress and success. They want to be recognized for their hard work and achievement (Employee of the Month, diplomas, awards) and to have ways of measuring their rise up the ranks. Social Threes are very adaptable, concerned with fitting into whatever culture they find themselves in, be it corporate or national. If they move to another country, they are able to adapt to the norms of that country more easily than most other types. If they join a spiritual community or ashram, they quickly become well adjusted to the social expectations of that community. The Social Threes are the most concerned with being appropriate and with avoiding any behaviors that would cause offense. At the same time, they are highly ambitious and so must balance their drive to excel and to surpass others with their desire to have others like and accept them.

Thus, of the three instinctual variants of this type, Social Threes are at the greatest risk of losing track of their core values and goals. They may adapt so successfully that they find themselves adrift without tangible goals or a clear path for achieving them. In this regard, they can resemble Sevens, moving from one promising project to another as they adapt to different opportunities that present themselves. Social Threes can also get into trouble by attempting to rise faster than they are able or by taking on tasks that they are not yet ready or qualified to perform. The desire to please and to impress can become a powerful magnet that can derail the Social Three from pursuing real, achievable goals.

Threes grow by recognizing that they do not need to separate their work and functioning from their feelings. Threes believe they will be less effective and competent if they allow their feelings to enter the picture. Thus, they wait until they are done with their tasks before they pay any attention to their emotions. Nonetheless, their emotions are always operating, even if unconsciously. And if Threes neglect them too long, those emotions start to make functioning much more difficult. Thus, growth for Threes entails pausing while working and actively checking in with their feelings. By tuning in to their heart and becoming more conscious of their inner life, Threes derive much greater happiness and satisfaction from their work and from their relationships.

See *Personality Types*, 95–133; *Understanding the Enneagram*, 43–46, 80–86, and 334–36; and *The Wisdom of the Enneagram*, 150–77.

9. Type Four: The Individualist

The Sensitive, Withdrawn Type: Expressive, Dramatic, Self-Absorbed, and Temperamental

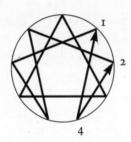

Generally, Fours are intuitive, sensitive, impressionable, quiet, introspective, passionate, romantic, elegant, witty, imaginative, and self-expressive.

Fours get into conflicts by being moody, emotionally demanding, self-absorbed, withholding, temperamental, dramatic, pretentious, and self-indulgent.

At their best, Fours are creative, inspired, honest with themselves, emotionally strong, humane, self-aware, discreet, and self-renewing.

Recognizing Fours

Type Four exemplifies the desire to be ourselves, to be known for who we are, and to know the depths of our own hearts. Of all the types, Fours are the most aware of their own emotional states. They notice when they feel upset, anxious, attracted to another person, or some other, more subtle combination of feelings. They pay attention to their different changing emotions and try to determine what their feelings are telling them about themselves, others, and their world. When Fours are more in balance, their exquisite attunement to their inner states enables them to discover deep truths about human nature, to bear compassionate witness to the suffering of others, or to be profoundly honest with themselves about their own motives. When they are less balanced, they can become lost in their feelings, preoccupied with emotional reactions, memories, and fantasies, both negative and positive.

Fours are nothing if not subtle and expressive, and they are able to put words to feelings and states that others may recognize but could not have expressed as eloquently. ("That poem exactly captures how I felt about leaving home.") By being emotionally honest, and by taking time to see what they really feel about things, they encourage others to look more deeply into themselves.

Fours are also people who care a great deal about beauty and taste. Many Fours, for instance, are involved in artistic pursuits. Even if they are not artistically creative themselves, Fours seek out art, poetry, music, and other expressions that they find beautiful, because they feel these things reveal something true about themselves and about human nature. Fours often dress in ways that accentuate their own sense of personal style but also in ways that symbolically let others know how they are feeling (dressing entirely in black or in shades of violet, for instance). Similarly, they typically decorate their homes with objects and colors that evoke a strong sense of image and mood and reflect personal feelings and associations.

Above all, Fours want to distinguish themselves from others — they want to feel that their taste, their self-expression, and their emotional depth are *unique*. Thus, they tend to emphasize all of the ways in which they are unlike other people — especially their own family. They deeply want to know who they are and that who they are is special in some way. Being complimented or told that they are loved is nice, of course, but what Fours really want is for others to recognize and appreciate the pattern of qualities that is unique *to them* — that they are not generic.

Because of their powerful need to see themselves as different from others, Fours often end up feeling alone and misunderstood. They become creative "outsiders," and they are proud of it. If they are working in a regular nine-to-five job, they will find ways to put their unique stamp on their work. This can run the gamut from finding their own way of presenting reports to having a recognizable design style to decorating their office in a way that reflects their tastes and feelings. They may run their own company (as long as there's a creative component to their work and it's emotionally satisfying), or they may be in a profession that makes use of their personal touch, such as a clothing designer, or counselor, or a therapist of some kind. Fours are often professional artists, writers, or teachers. Above all, Fours *want their life to be a work of art*. They want to achieve something beautiful despite the loneliness, suffering, and self-doubt they have so often felt.

Unfortunately, the Four's need to be different can also lead to alienation and a tendency to become engrossed in feelings of loss, sadness, and melancholy. All nine types can feel sad, lonely, or depressed, but Fours feel this way frequently — even when there is nothing in their current lives to cause such feelings. They often become convinced that these painful feelings are more real and authentic when compared to more passing feelings of happiness or enthusiasm. Indeed, Fours begin to feel that they are being the most real, most honest people *because* they are focusing on disappointment and sadness. Ultimately, this can lead them to foster and prolong these painful feelings in themselves.

In brief, Fours want to express themselves and their individuality, to create and surround themselves with beauty, to maintain certain moods and feelings, to withdraw and protect their vulnerabilities, to take care of emotional needs before attending to anything else, and to attract a "rescuer" who will understand them. **Fours do not want** to restrain or lose touch with their emotions, to feel ordinary, to have their individuality go unrecognized, to have their taste questioned, to be *required* in social settings, to follow impersonal rules and procedures, or to spend time with people they perceive as lacking taste or emotional depth.

Their Hidden Side

On the surface, Fours can seem to suffer from chronic self-doubt and extreme sensitivity to others' reactions to them. But part of the reason for this is that Fours often hold a secret, inner image of who they feel they *could* be. They have an idea of the sort of person they would like to become, the kind of person who would be fantastically talented, socially adept, and intensely desired. In short, Fours come to believe that if they were somehow different from who they are, they would be seen and loved. Unfortunately, they constantly compare themselves negatively to this idealized secret self — their "fantasy self." This makes it very difficult for Fours to appreciate many of their genuine positive qualities because they are never as wonderful as the fantasy. Much of the growth for type Four involves letting go of this idealized secret self so that they can see and appreciate who they actually are.

Relationship Issues

As the romantics of the Enneagram, Fours focus a great deal of their time and attention on their relationships. High-functioning Fours are sensitive to others — especially to others' feelings — and enjoy any kind of authentic personal sharing. They are excellent listeners and give their full attention when someone they care about is trying to express herself. Unfortunately, Fours also tend to get caught up in their own emotional reactions and dramas. When this happens, they have difficulty seeing others or hearing them objectively. Their strong emotional reactions can make it difficult for them to sustain interpersonal connections. Fours tend to have the following issues in relationships:

- Becoming self-absorbed and uninterested in others' feelings or problems due to feeling overwhelmed by their own feelings.
- Idealizing potential partners, then feeling disappointed once they get to know them — often devaluing and rejecting them.

- Placing great expectations on the partner for nurturing and support.
- Being moody and temperamental — making others "walk on eggshells."
- Withholding attention and affection to punish the other.
- Imagining that others have worse opinions of them than they do — being touchy and hypersensitive to slights.

The Passion: Envy

At some level, Fours believe that they are missing something that other people seem to have. They feel that something is wrong with them or with their relationships, and they start to be acutely aware of what is *not* working in their lives. Naturally, given this frame of mind, it is difficult for Fours to feel good about themselves or to appreciate the good things in their world.

Fours rightly perceive that there is something inadequate or incomplete about the ego self, but *they incorrectly assume that they alone suffer from this problem.* Fours then get in the habit of comparing themselves to others, concluding that they have somehow gotten "the short end of the stick." Fours feel that they have been singled out by fate for bad treatment, bad luck, unsatisfying relationships, bad parenting, and broken dreams. It comes as something of a shock to many Fours to discover that other people have suffered as much or even more than they have. This doesn't mean that Fours haven't suffered or that their painful pasts are inconsequential. But Fours need to see how they perpetuate their own suffering by continually focusing on old wounds rather than truly processing those hurts and letting go of them in a way that would allow them to heal.

At Their Best

Healthy Fours strive to be true to themselves. They are emotionally honest and aren't afraid to reveal themselves to others, "warts and all." They combine self-awareness and introspection with great emotional strength and endurance. They bring a heightened sensitivity to their experiences and are able to share with others the subtleties of their inner world. This invites others to do the same. They are highly intuitive and creative and add a personal, human touch to whatever they are involved with. They treat others with gentleness, tact, and discretion. They can be wonderfully expressive with an ironic, witty view of life and themselves, often finding humor in their own foibles and contradictions. They bring a sense of beauty, refinement, and emotional richness into other people's lives.

Thus, high-functioning Fours are profoundly creative, expressing the personal and the universal, possibly through art but also in their daily lives. They are in touch with the ever-changing nature of reality and are inspired by it. High-functioning Fours are able to renew and regenerate themselves again and again, transforming even their most painful experiences into something beautiful and meaningful that others can benefit from as well. They have a deep sense of "allowing," and they are able to hold even the most painful feelings with compassion and sensitivity — whether their own or someone else's.

Personality Dynamics and Variations

Under Stress (Four Goes to Average Two)

Fours attempt to defend their hurt feelings (and gain attention) by withdrawing from people and withholding their own affection and attention. They may recognize on some level, however, that their emotional storminess and withdrawals are driving away the people who are most supportive of them. Then Fours go out of their way to reestablish their connections and reassure themselves that their relationship is still on solid ground. But because they are reacting out of stress, Fours may overcompensate by trying to win others over, by doing favors, or, more darkly, by manipulation and creating dependencies, all in the manner of average-to-unhealthy Twos. To do this, they keep talking about the state of the relationship with the other person and try to make themselves more needed. Favors, help, and reminding others of their support are part of the picture. Troubled Fours also become more possessive of loved ones, not wanting to let them out of their sight for long, like lower-functioning Twos.

Security (Four goes to Average One)

With trusted intimates, or in situations in which Fours feel sure of themselves, they may risk being more openly controlling and critical of others. Their frustration with others and disappointment in how others are behaving (especially toward them) finally erupts. Fours can become impatient and critical, demanding that people meet their exacting standards, constantly pointing out how others have made errors. Nothing about the other person (whom they may have idealized and regarded as their longed-for "rescuer") now satisfies them or gives them much hope or pleasure. Everything about the person and their situation becomes irritating and annoying and they can't seem to get the other person's faults out of their mind. Fours in this state may also compensate for their ragged emotions by driving themselves excessively, feeling that they are lazy and unproductive if they are not constantly working and improving.

Integration (Four Goes to Healthy One)

As Fours become more aware of their tendency to brood and to fantasize about their many hurts and disappointments, they also become aware of the cost to themselves of this way of being. As they relax and accept themselves more deeply, they gradually become free of their constant emotional turbulence and their need to maintain emotional crises or to indulge themselves as a consolation prize for not fulfilling their potential. Gradually and naturally, they become more objective, grounded, and practical, like healthy Ones. They also become more realistic and able to operate in the real world. Without imposing harsh disciplines or expectations on themselves, integrating Fours want to become involved in matters beyond themselves, such as community work, politics, the environment, or in other worthwhile ways to engage their minds and hearts. On some level, they choose no longer to indulge themselves but to live within the constraints of reality.

When they do so, they find the payoffs and the pleasures — and their creativity — are deeper and much more fulfilling.

The Instincts in Brief

Self-Preservation Fours: The Sensualist (Ichazo's "Reckless/Dauntless")

Self-Preservation Fours focus their envy and hypersensitivity on their concerns about their immediate environment and on their quest for physical comfort. They attempt to deal with emotional issues by surrounding themselves with as much luxury and beauty as they can afford, by indulging in their favorite foods, and by giving themselves "consolation prizes" for their suffering. They might be disappointed about a job situation or a failing relationship, and so stay up late at night drinking expensive cognac and watching a favorite movie. Self-Pres Fours are particularly sensitive to comfort issues — the temperature of a room, the quality of the lighting, the humidity or lack of it, the weather — all produce powerful *emotional* responses. Self-Pres Fours become frustrated that the environment is insufficiently attuned to their personal needs. Attempts to control the environment and self-indulgence in rich foods, drink, drugs, or other sensual distractions can exhaust Self-Pres Fours, leaving them unable to function well outside of their own narrowing world.

Sexual Fours: Infatuation (Ichazo's "Competition")

Sexual Fours focus their envy and hypersensitivity in their intimate relationships. They are perhaps the most emotionally intense type of the Enneagram, which is both their gift and their potential downfall. They possess both a capacity and a desire for profound intimacy, and they derive tremendous insight into human nature through the ups and downs of their romantic lives. They have a sultry, sullen quality that can be attractive and mysterious, or at times, off-putting to others. Sexual Fours pour their energy and attention into the object of their affection, often becoming infatuated or even obsessed, sometimes after only one meeting. Sexual chemistry triggers their powerful imaginations, leading them to create enormous expectations of potential partners. Sexual Fours tend to be drawn to people who possess qualities and talents that they believe they lack. They want to complete themselves by associating or merging with the valued other. But this almost never works, so they may also end up envying and resenting their romantic partner for unintentionally reminding them of what they feel they are missing. In any case, Sexual Fours go through tremendous shifts of feeling about their loved ones — everything from idolization to unbridled hatred. Generally speaking, this type is aware of these feelings, including the dark ones, and expresses them, sometimes in self-destructive ways.

Social Fours: The Outsider (Ichazo's "Social Shame")

Social Fours focus their envy and hypersensitivity in the social realm; thus, they are people who deeply want to belong, to be a part of an "in crowd" with a glamorous lifestyle, but who often fear that they are not up to it. Social Fours tend to be more extroverted than Fours of the other two instincts and can resemble Twos or Sevens. Social Fours can be quite funny, using droll, ironic humor to make a point or simply to stimulate conversation. They enjoy expressing their individuality and sense of style in a more public way, although they also attempt to conceal the extent of their feelings of social inadequacy or shame. Social Fours may work hard to develop a public persona through which they can communicate the depths of their feelings, but this persona is usually more glamorous and free than they actually feel. Social Fours are acutely aware of the artifice of their persona, but they use it nonetheless as a way of finding some sense of belonging and involvement in the world. When they are more troubled, Social Fours fear social humiliation to such a degree that they may retreat from much social contact, becoming isolated and reclusive. They may also develop a personal style cultivated to show the world how wounded and different they feel.

Fours grow by recognizing that while the hurts and losses of the past were real enough, there is no need to keep revisiting them in the imagination. On the contrary, doing so keeps drawing them out of the richness and depth of the present moment — the one time and place in which their real feelings and their true identity can be found. Fours need to see how working up their feelings actually moves them further away from their most authentic self and their truest self-expression.

See also *Personality Types*, 134–72; *Understanding the Enneagram*, 46–49, 86–92, and 337–39; and *The Wisdom of the Enneagram*, 177–205.

10. Type Five: The Investigator

The Intense, Cerebral Type: Perceptive, Innovative, Secretive, and Isolated

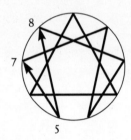

Generally, Fives are focused, observant, curious, insightful, expert, studious, complex, profound, perceptive, whimsical, unsentimental, exploratory, and independent.

Fives get into conflicts by being detached, preoccupied, highstrung, isolated, impractical, unconventional, uncompromising, extreme, and provocative.

At their best, Fives are visionary, pioneering, innovative, objective, understanding, playful, compassionate, and nonattached.

Recognizing Fives

Type Five exemplifies the human desire to understand, to look beneath the surface of things, and to arrive at deeper insights about reality. Fives prefer the life of the mind, both as a way of understanding the world and — given the unlimited power of imagination — as a way of escaping from aspects of reality. It would not be far-fetched to say that for many Fives, the inner world of the mind and the imagination is more real and vivid than the external world. Fives tend to have an experience and then spend many hours, days — even years — understanding it and its broader context. Fives are also highly innovative and inventive. They love "tinkering around," playing with concepts and overturning the accepted ways of doing things. This can produce extremely valuable, practical, and original works and discoveries or simply entertain them for many hours with no practical results.

Fives are truly the most independent and idiosyncratic of the personality types, the people who could most appropriately be called "loners" and "misfits." They are people who truly march to a different drummer, pursuing their interests and curiosity wherever their investigations may take them. Some Fives can seem downright odd to people while others keep their "weirdness" more below the surface. In either case, Fives are intensely determined to pursue the questions and ideas that fascinate them: so much so that relationships and financial considerations can become unimportant to them.

These qualities result from an extraordinary ability to focus their attention. Fives will stay with a problem or a question that fascinates them until it is solved, or until they discover that it is unsolvable. Boredom is unimaginable to them because there are so many fascinating things to explore, understand, and imagine. The downside is that their capacity for concentration enables them to get deeply engrossed in their complex inner worlds, sometimes to the extent that they forget their surroundings or even to take care of themselves.

Thus, Fives can get involved in work, reading, or in their own thoughts in such depth that they are often late for meetings and don't hear phone calls. They forget to eat or to take adequate care of themselves physically. They will live on soda and candy bars, or stay up all night writing a story or trying to solve an interesting problem. They will pore over the computer terminal for hours, or disappear into the stacks of the local library, only to emerge five minutes before closing with an armload of books as they head to the nearest coffee shop to continue reading.

But this doesn't mean that Fives always want to be alone or that they can't be excellent company when they are with others.

When Fives find someone whose intelligence and interest they respect, they are invariably talkative and sociable. Fives love to share their insights and expertise with just about anyone who appreciates what they have to say. They also enjoy sharing their findings with others, and their observations of life's contradictions and absurdities are often served up with a whimsical sense of humor. Fives can be the most enriching of friends since they are a treasure trove of information, speculation, opinions, and intensely felt ideas. But they can also be the most impenetrable of enigmas, a mind bristling with energy and intelligence that signals "Stay away! Leave me alone to follow my thoughts wherever they may lead!" Fives are the kind of people others usually find strange, quirky, and intriguing — they always have more going on than meets the eye.

In brief, Fives want to understand reality, to possess knowledge, to find a niche for themselves that others have not explored, to be free to explore their own inner worlds, to have sufficient solitude and time for their projects, to feel confident and capable, and to unsettle the unquestioned certainties of others. *Fives do not want* to feel uninformed or incapable, to have their competency questioned, to accept easy answers, to be intruded on (or "managed"), to be forced to respond before they feel ready, to suffer the ignorance of others, or to ask for help.

Their Hidden Side

Day for day, even socially adept Fives probably spend more time by themselves than any other type. Nonetheless, Fives need companionship and connection as do all human beings. The problem is that Fives fear needing the affection and warmth of others. It as if they feel that to ask for anything from others is to risk a greater imposition on their own freedom and independence. They also believe that their own needs are so intense that if they were ever expressed or even acknowledged, they would be too much for others. In some cases, they may even believe that their needs would actually harm others. Deep down, all Fives really want to find someone safe to connect with, but they fear that doing so will cost them whatever degree of competency and self-reliance they have attained. If troubled Fives feel that their area of mastery or their independence is at risk, they may retreat from a relationship — even if they truly love the person they are leaving.

Relationship Issues

Of all the types, Fives seem most able to live *without* significant relationships. But that doesn't mean that they do not want one, only that they are generally unwilling to compromise their focused approach to life too much for the sake of a relationship. When they find someone who understands their world, who appreciates their interests, and whom they respect, Fives are loyal and passionate friends, partners, and lovers. They can make fascinating companions who are constantly introducing new ideas to their friends and partners. They can be funny, affectionate, and highly sexual, but they do not come to relationships easily. They remain in an uneasy balance between the desire for solitude and the desire for meaningful connection. Fives' relationship issues include the following:

- Frequently feeling intruded on and therefore needing a great deal of privacy and time alone.
- Often feeling rejected and retreating from people.
- Being overwhelmed by others' emotional needs.
- Not expressing their feelings or giving few verbal or nonverbal cues, thus seeming overly "secretive" to others.
- Antagonizing or undermining the calm or beliefs of others.
- Cutting off contact with people, withdrawing into deep isolation, feeling that they are "poisonous" or bad for people.

The Passion: Avarice (or Hoarding)

Beneath the surface image of intellectual competency that Fives present to the world, this type feels small and helpless. They feel as if there is not enough of themselves to go around and that other people's needs could easily deplete them. Thus, Fives seek to minimize their interactions with others and with the environment and to hold on to whatever basic resources they think they will need to "go it alone." Avarice is not the grasping of gluttonous Sevens; rather, it is the lack of ability to be open and generous with one's self because of fears of not being enough. Another way avarice is expressed in Fives is in the desire to memorize experiences and knowledge. Fives attempt to hold every potentially significant piece of information they have encountered in their heads, believing that eventually they will know enough to feel confident and able to handle any possible situation.

At Their Best

Healthy Fives observe everything with extraordinary perceptiveness and insight. Possessing a searching intelligence, they are highly mentally alert and curious: little escapes their notice. Healthy Fives are able to concentrate deeply and often notice things that other people would likely overlook or take for granted. They explore reality with a child's sense of wonder and enjoy finding new ways of perceiving and doing things. They like to ask questions, and with healthy Fives, they are often the right questions. They enjoy learning and are excited by knowledge, which frequently leads them to become expert in some field. Because of their focus and attentiveness, healthy Fives attain mastery in whatever interests them.

Very high-functioning Fives become visionaries and discoverers, broadly comprehending the world while penetrating it profoundly. They are remarkably open-minded, understanding things precisely and as a whole. They begin to feel a deep connection with their fellow human beings and with the universe, and they often dedicate themselves to using their skill and knowledge to relieve human suffering and ignorance. They may contribute pioneering discoveries of something entirely new for the enrichment of humanity. At their best, Fives combine the wisdom and perceptiveness of their minds with heart and courage in ways that truly bring something new and valuable into the world.

Personality Dynamics and Variations

Under Stress (Five Goes to Average Seven)

Fives usually cope with difficulties by retreating into their minds where they feel more confident and in control. But Fives cannot retreat indefinitely, and eventually they need stimulation and interaction. Fives also tend to be nervous and high-strung, so when there is no outlet for their nervous energy, it builds up, eventually expressing itself in restlessness and hyperactivity. (Fives can become literally "restless" and often develop insomnia.) Anxiety causes their minds to overheat and to jump from one thought to the next. Much of their characteristic focus gets scattered. After being alone and concentrating for so long, they begin to overcompensate by overdoing their activities and lurching from one promising idea or experience to another. They become like a starving person at a banquet, and their scattered, hyperactive behavior can look like that of an average Seven. At such times, usually quiet Fives may become very talkative, impulsive, and flighty. Their underlying anxiety gets acted out in compulsive, even manic, behavior in ways that resemble lower-functioning Sevens.

Security (Five Goes to Average Eight)

Most often, if Fives feel that others are intruding on them or imposing their wills, they will simply leave quietly if they can or shut down into a detached, disdainful silence. With people or situations in which they have more confidence, however, Fives may suddenly risk behaving like average Eights, forcefully asserting their boundaries and confronting anyone or anything that displeases them. They become feisty, argumentative, and relentlessly provocative. In this mode they take a tough stance, putting everyone on notice that they cannot be trifled with, but in ways that often cause people to react against them. They may become domineering and even aggressive, while questioning others' competence.

Integration (Five Goes to Healthy Eight)

As Fives begin to understand the emotional cost of their self-imposed isolation, they begin to risk deeper, more complete contact with themselves and with the world. They become more grounded, more in touch with their bodies and their life energy, giving them more confidence and solidity. As this process deepens, integrating Fives naturally begin to express many qualities of the healthy Eight: they demonstrate leadership, courage, practical wisdom, and the willingness to take responsibility. They move from feeling small and powerless to feeling grounded and capable. Their knowledge and insight are then in service to objective needs in their world, and they are sought by others as sources of wisdom, compassion, and quiet strength.

The Instincts in Brief

Self-Preservation Fives: Isolation (Ichazo's "Castle")

Self-Preservation Fives are the most introverted Fives — the Fives most likely to seek long periods of privacy and solitude. The hoarding of the Five is focused in the areas of practical resources, living quarters, and personal space. Self-Pres Fives attempt to find out how *few* self-preservation needs they can subsist on, likely agreeing with Thoreau's statement that "A man is rich in proportion to what he can do without." They are intensely private people who seem to require few comforts, even if they have substantial personal wealth. To some degree, they enjoy the company of trusted others and enjoy sharing their knowledge with people. They can also be counted on for their sense of whimsy and oddball humor. Nonetheless, Self-Pres Fives need lots of time by themselves to regenerate their energy. Many choose to live alone, or if they are in a partnership, they require personal space (such as a study or a nook in the basement) into which others, even loved ones, will not intrude. They also tend to hoard personal effects, stockpiling their homes like castles preparing for a siege. As much as they may like and admire others, they attempt to keep their relationships few and simple, so that they can focus on what holds interest for them.

Sexual Fives: This Is My World (Ichazo's "Confidence")

Sexual Fives focus their hoarding in the area of intimate relationships. The combination of instinct and type are at odds here: the Five defense is to withdraw, while the sexual instinct demands intimacy and connection. Most Sexual Fives live in an uneasy truce between these polar influences, but they seek to resolve this tension by slowly inviting prospective intimates into their own secret world. Sexual Fives are primarily focused in their imaginations, but they believe that most others would find their thoughts and preoccupations dark and even frightening. At the very least, they are certain that others will find them odd or eccentric. Nonetheless, they want to share their perceptions and hidden worlds and secretly hope to have a deep connection with a single soul, a mate for life, who can understand them and their sometimes bizarre views of reality. Intimacy for them entails finding someone else who will explore the surreal vistas of their inner world. They also look to their partner for some degree of help in dealing with people and the practical affairs of life. They hope that their partner will run interference for them and give them confidence to navigate the external world. If Sexual Fives are disappointed in love, they may retreat and remain unattached for long periods of time, even years. *So true*

Social Fives: The Specialist (Ichazo's "Totems")

Social Fives focus their avarice and hoarding in the social realm, meaning that they socialize through their particular areas of expertise. Fives endeavor to master some skill or body of knowledge, and they relate to others primarily through that area of their mastery. As social types, Social Fives are more comfortable interacting with people, but their comfort is largely dependent on having a context for being in a social situation. They need a particular task or function that gives them the confidence to interact with people (for example, being the DJ at a party, or having a specific topic of discussion at a social event). They enjoy talking intensely with other people who share their (sometimes esoteric) interests — either in person or through the Internet. Social Fives feel that their expertise is what they can "bring to the table" since they make it their business to learn things that others may need. While generally quiet, Social Fives can become quite talkative if their area of knowledge becomes the topic of conversation; anything from computer expertise to trivia about movies or comic books is fair game. Less healthy Social Fives can become elitist, feeling others are too unintelligent to understand their thoughts or conversation. They can also be fiercely argumentive, losing social connections by reactively proving others' ideas inadequate.

Fives grow by recognizing that real confidence lies not simply in intellectual mastery but in putting themselves out into the world. Fives usually derive their confidence through the development of their minds, but they really need to bring balance to their psyches by developing a deeper relationship with their bodies and feelings. Fives actually feel things deeply, but they are extremely restrained in their ability to express their feelings. Growth for Fives requires allowing themselves to see how estranged they are from their actual living selves and acknowledging all of the deep needs that they have denied since early childhood. Developing trust of others, sharing what they are experiencing, and identifying with their feelings are all crucial for them to blossom fully as human beings. All of this becomes much easier when Fives are grounded in their bodies.

See also *Personality Types*, 173–215; *Understanding the Enneagram*, 49–52, 92–98, and 339–41; and *The Wisdom of the Enneagram*, 206–32.

11. Type Six: The Loyalist

The Committed, Security-Oriented Type:
Engaging, Responsible, Anxious, and
Suspicious

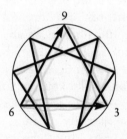

Generally, Sixes are reliable, hard-working, organizing, vigilant, dutiful, evaluating, persevering, cautious, anxious, believing *and* doubting, conservative *and* liberal.

Sixes get into conflicts by being pessimistic, defensive, evasive, negative, worrying, doubtful, negativistic, reactive, suspicious, and blaming.

At their best, Sixes are courageous, cooperative, disciplined, grounded, secure, faithful, self-expressive, funny, and affectionate.

Recognizing Sixes

Type Six exemplifies the desire to create a stable, safe environment, to cooperate and create with others, and to be adequately prepared for the various difficulties that life presents. Sixes are meticulous, disciplined, and persevering. They are good with details, and they have a talent for seeing potential problems and dealing with them before they get out of hand. They organize resources, prioritize tasks, and see projects through. Sixes are not necessarily "group people," but they like the feeling of "belonging" somewhere — of being part of something greater than themselves. They enjoy being of service and really want to contribute to the world. They bring reliability, responsibility, hard work, and a sense of honor to all their affairs. They approach others as if to say, "I am here for you. You can count on me."

Sixes do their best to be solid and responsible, but they are often troubled by an undercurrent of doubt and anxiety. In fact, Sixes often seem a bit jittery and uneasy in general. They live in a state of worry — and *then find something to worry about.* They often "scan" their surroundings for problems, expecting that something negative could happen at any time. Consequently, they are usually careful about the management of their affairs, and generally cautious in their dealings with others. At the same time, they are always on the lookout for someone they *can* trust, someone they can rely on. Because it takes them a while to feel confident that someone is truly on their side, Sixes will sometimes "test" people by provoking them in some way to see how they will react. Once they have decided that someone has passed the test, there is almost no limit to their loyalty or to the sacrifices that Sixes will make for the sake of the trusted person.

Sixes know that once they make a commitment, they do so 110 percent. They find it difficult to leave a relationship once they have begun to trust someone and to rely on that person. Thus, they want to be sure that they are putting their energies into someone who will be there for them consistently. Once they have established a solid relationship, they show their trust and affection by supporting the other person in every way they can, especially by being reliable and trustworthy themselves.

One sign that Sixes have issues with trust is that they approach others with a sincere but *cautious* friendliness. When Sixes are relaxed, they have a natural talent for engaging people and for finding common ground. They often get others to like them by joking around and bantering, and through other forms of physical and social bonding. They want to find things about people that are familiar and that they can relate to — looking for common interests and experiences that would be the basis of trust. They tend to get nervous in situations in which they do not know where others stand — where there are too many unknowns, too many unfamiliar elements.

Fundamentally, Sixes are looking for someone to trust because they do not really trust themselves. They do not have much faith in themselves and their own abilities, so they look outside themselves to a person, a job, an authority figure, or a belief system of some sort for guidance and security. This doesn't solve their insecurity in the long run, however, because the more Sixes rely on others for their confidence, the more self-doubting and insecure they become. They will keep bouncing back and forth between depending on others and trying to prove that they are tough and independent themselves.

Some Sixes tend to collapse into their anxiety more often, feeling fearful, anxious, dependent, and openly seeking support from others. These are called "phobic Sixes." Other Sixes are more apt to impulsively leap into activities connected with their fears — such as a person with a fear of heights who decides to take up rock climbing, or a person who fears authority figures becoming a spokesperson for an antiestablishment group. These are called "counterphobic Sixes." In truth, all Sixes have both phobic and counterphobic aspects, and they express their different responses in different areas of their lives. A Six might be phobic around her boss, for instance, but behave counterphobically with her spouse.

In brief, Sixes want to have security, to feel supported by others, to have certitude and reassurance, to test the attitudes of others toward them, to fight against anxiety and insecurity, and they prefer predictability as a way of defending the self from threats from the environment. **Sixes do not want** to feel abandoned, to have uncertainty, to have contradictory expectations placed on them, to feel pressured, to have to accept new ideas rapidly, to work with people who they feel are not carrying their weight, or to have their security systems and beliefs questioned, especially by anyone they see as an outsider.

Their Hidden Side

Sixes seem like highly organized and responsible people and can often resemble Ones. But the hidden problem is that Sixes are trying to calm their inner anxieties by trying to make their external world trouble-free and predictable. Of course, this is ultimately an impossible task, but Sixes still usually persevere in the effort to make their world safe from danger and mishaps.

The real source of anxiety in Sixes is internal and is perpetuated by their constantly turning thoughts. In short, Sixes cannot stop second-guessing themselves, doubting what they know, and consulting what amounts to an "inner committee" of contrary voices. ("Did I get the electric bill out this morning? Yes. I think so. Good. But what did I forget. Oh yes! I was supposed to call Maggie about lunch tomorrow. She is going to be so angry with me. Should I call her now or is it too late?") With their minds revved up in a hypervigilant state, it is almost impossible for Sixes to relax so that they can perceive clearly how to attend to the actual challenges they need to address at any given time. What Sixes really need is more inner quiet. They need to cultivate a sense of peace and inner quiet that would allow them to see and deal with reality more clearly.

Relationship Issues

Sixes can be confusing to others (and themselves) in relationships because they seem so changeable and unpredictable. In one moment, they feel nervous and want to be reassured that their partner is really on board with them. They want to know that the other person is close and available. In the next moment, they can easily feel smothered or overwhelmed by their partner and want to create some distance in the relationship. A moment later, they are looking for reassurance that they haven't gone too far in being independent. In short, Sixes are seeking what psychologists call "optimal distance." They want to keep their loved ones close enough so that they will not feel abandoned but not so close that they feel engulfed by the other person.

Relationship issues for Sixes include the following:

- Testing the other person to see if he or she is going to stay.
- Getting overcommitted, causing Sixes to feel pressured and taken advantage of.
- Either "clamming up" and not expressing their feelings or venting a stream of anxieties.
- Alternating between feeling dependent and needy at one extreme and feeling defiant and rebellious at the other — running "hot or cold."
- Easily becoming suspicious, reflexively doubting the goodwill of others toward them.
- Blaming people for the Six's own anxieties and projecting negative motivations onto others.

The Passion: Anxiety (Traditionally "Fear")

The passion of the Six is often described as fear, but fear is an organic response to a real danger in our environment. Anxiety, on the other hand, is the *anticipation* of a danger or a problem. It is a sense of dread and a capacity to continually conjure worst-case scenarios in our imagination. Thus, Sixes are habitually on the lookout for potential disasters with the result that their minds are constantly agitated. Ultimately, this can leave them less prepared to deal with real problems because they are making themselves fearful *imagining* what could go wrong. The more anxious Sixes become, the more their minds become worked up, and the less they are able to access the quiet, inner knowing that would give them clarity about what to do.

The passion of type Six can also be expressed as *doubt*. Sixes seldom trust their own minds, their own capacity to know, when they are in the grip of doubt. They second-guess themselves, rechecking math they are sure they did correctly, going back to the house to make sure that they locked the door that they actually remember locking, and so forth. As we have seen, Sixes are anxious to have reliable sources of support and guidance in their lives, be they books, friends, advisors, philosophies, jobs, or anything else. But once doubt sets in, Sixes doubt that these very support systems will be there for them. They question even their most ardent supporters as their doubt gives way to growing suspicion or even paranoia.

At Their Best

Healthy Sixes are able to elicit strong emotional responses from others: they are engaging, friendly, and playful — truly likable, dependable people. They bring a sense of trust and camaraderie to their relationships and treat everyone — including themselves — as an equal. They are strongly committed and loyal to the people in their lives, and they work hard to build stability, security, and prosperity in their homes, jobs, and communities. Healthy Sixes are the foundation of any society. They believe in cooperation and shared goals, helping to organize people and tackle problems. They bring a democratic approach to their dealings with others and will fight for the powerless and disenfranchised as they would for themselves.

High-functioning Sixes become self-confident and self-affirming. They trust themselves and have learned self-reliance and independence because they know that they are deeply grounded in the limitless support of Being. Faith in this inner support and sense of guidance leads to a positive, life-affirming attitude, often manifesting itself as outstanding courage and leadership. High-functioning Sixes combine a commitment to being guided by their own inner knowing with a commitment to allowing themselves to be led wherever the truth takes them. As a result, they can become powerful influences for the greater good.

Personality Dynamics and Variations

Under Stress (Six Goes to Average Three)

Sixes are often visibly nervous, reacting with self-doubt to situations and getting caught in overthinking a problem. When stress escalates beyond the normal level, however, they jump into action — and stay in action, trying to deal with their anxieties by working harder. If, for example, they feel pressured at work, Sixes may spend their weekend frantically doing yard chores or obsessively reorganizing the closets as a way of discharging or avoiding feelings of inadequacy. They also fear letting others know how overwhelmed they are, so they may take on a false persona of competency and efficiency, like average Threes. ("Don't worry about anything, I've got this handled.") They focus increasingly on tasks and on being efficient while cutting off from their feelings so that they can stay functional, but this can lead to major emotional problems for them and for their relationships.

Security (Six Goes to Average Nine)

In situations where Sixes feel secure, they begin to deal with stress by simply shutting down and becoming indifferent to their surroundings, like average Nines. They do not want to be disturbed or bothered by loved ones — they feel that they have been working hard and they experience virtually any kind of interaction as another source of pressure. They will be pleasant one moment, but can suddenly become stubbornly resistant and shut down in the next if they feel that others are demanding something of them. At such times, Sixes become unavailable and passive-aggressive, not wanting to respond to others or to move out of comforting but numbing routines.

Integration (Six Goes to Healthy Nine)

As Sixes learn to trust themselves more, they also become more open to life and to other people. They gradually learn to relax their hypervigilance and simply *be* with themselves or with whatever life is presenting in the moment. They gain a deeper acceptance of life's ups and downs such that they are not riddled with dread and anxiety. They are inclusive and supportive of others — and much more at peace. Integrating Sixes are able to let their minds rest in their natural, pristine state of clarity and inner quiet. They are able to stop second-guessing everything and let their own inner wisdom arise. The result is that they are more serene, grounded, and joyous — light and stable.

The Instincts in Brief

Self-Preservation Sixes: Responsibility (Ichazo's "Affection")

Self-Preservation Sixes find their security through safeguarding resources — money, food, property, shelter, and so forth — and tend to chronically worry about these things. ("Have the bills been paid?" "Have the car's brakes been checked recently?" "Do we have enough insurance?") They care a great deal about safety and thrift. Indeed, Self-Pres Sixes feel most secure when they are responsible for financial matters and believe that their effective running of these affairs is something they can contribute. When they are less secure, however, they do not trust others to be responsible. They need to be constantly informed, if not entirely in control, of practical matters that affect them. Self-Pres Sixes can be funny and friendly and want to be involved and engaged, but they have difficulty relaxing, especially around unfamiliar others. They are more introverted and more likely to be loners than the other Sixes. When more stressed, they may stay in punishing situations longer than they should (bad jobs, bad marriages) or become concerned with having control of resources, like a less healthy Eight.

Sexual Sixes: Feisty Vulnerablilty (Ichazo's "Strength and Beauty")

Sexual Sixes get their sense of security primarily from their emotional bond with a significant other. But they also have many doubts, both about their own ability to have a suitable mate and about the mate's ability or willingness to really be there for them. Moreover, Sexual Sixes often manifest a tension between their gender roles: they are both masculine and feminine, "macho" and coquettish. Sexual Six women have a tough, tomboy side to them

but still come across as feminine. Similarly, the men of this variant display a sensitivity and vulnerability while being essentially
masculine. Sexual Sixes also tend to be emotionally intense, like
Eights and Fours. Part of this comes from anxiety about their ability to keep a strong, capable partner. Thus, Sexual Sixes try to cultivate their masculine or feminine attributes in order to find a
good partner and, later, to remain appealing to this person. Often,
they feel most comfortable relating to members of the opposite
sex and may feel competitive with the opposite sex. They also
tend to test their significant others to see if they are strong enough
and to make sure that they are really committed to the relationship. When more stressed, Sexual Sixes can be emotionally volatile, with their feelings about people changing strongly and suddenly. They fall into suspiciousness about their partner and can be
quite jealous, while at the same time feeling a strong need to continue to "prove" their desirability.

Social Sixes: Generating Support (Ichazo's "Duty")

Social Sixes look for security in the social sphere — that is,
through their affiliations with different people and organizations.
They are warm, engaging, and humorous, trying to send out the
message that they are approachable and safe. They like to enlist
people, getting others involved in projects or activities they see as
worthwhile. Social Sixes frequently volunteer to work in groups
and committees. They do not necessarily *enjoy* doing this, but
they see it is necessary and so are willing to give their time and
energy. They want to be regarded as regular guys or gals and may
have difficulty taking stands that would be unpopular in their
peer groups. They seek consensus before moving ahead with their
agendas and want to feel that others are "with them," backing
them up. Although Social Sixes like being involved, they often become nervous about holding positions of responsibility because
they are afraid that they will have to make decisions that others
will not like, thus losing their support. When more insecure, their
suspiciousness may lead them to form in-groups and out-groups
in the workplace or in other social or societal areas.

Sixes grow by recognizing that the only real security in life comes from within. While we can work hard to build our finances, to find the right friends and the right partner, and to foresee every possible mishap, ultimately, none of the external structures that we use to give ourselves confidence will *always* work for us. Things can and do go wrong, and the supports that we rely on inevitably change. Therefore, growth for a Six entails finding the support of their own inner knowing. It involves finding the place inside themselves that is quiet, strong, and capable. But this cannot happen by itself. Discovering these inner resources takes time and work, although, fortunately, Sixes understand the usefulness of perseverance and dedication. Sixes will know firsthand the value of discovering their inner resources when they take time to relax their constant vigilance and find faith in themselves.

See *Personality Types*, 216–58; *Understanding the Enneagram*, 52–54, 98–105, and 341–44; and *The Wisdom of the Enneagram*, 233–59.

12. Type Seven: The Enthusiast

The Busy, Fun-Loving Type: Spontaneous, Versatile, Distractible, and Scattered

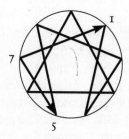

Generally, Sevens are excitable, spontaneous, curious, optimistic, eager, outgoing, future-oriented, adventurous, variety-seeking, quick, and talkative.

Sevens get into conflicts by being scattered, distracted, restless, impatient, thrill-seeking, escapist, overextended, irresponsible, demanding, and excessive.

At their best, Sevens are appreciative, bountiful, thoughtful, accomplished, versatile, receptive, grateful, quiet, and passionate.

Recognizing Sevens

Type Seven exemplifies the desire for freedom and variety and for exploring the many rich experiences that life offers. Thus, Sevens are probably the most enthusiastic, extroverted, and outgoing type of the Enneagram. They are spontaneous and upbeat; they find life exhilarating. They are the kind of people who make ordinary life into a celebration. Sevens like to fill up their calendar with things to do: after work, a quick drink; then off to dinner and

145

the theater; then after that, a nightcap before getting home at 2 A.M. The next night may bring the symphony, a ball game, singing in the local choir, or a visit to a new restaurant. Sevens who do not live in large cities or who do not have enough money for that diverse a lifestyle might have to make do with less lavishness. But they still seek variety and constant experience, whether it's going to a mall or out to a movie, talking on the phone with friends, hanging out in a bar, or leafing through magazines and daydreaming about a vacation. Sevens do their best to stay up on what's new, and so their wide-ranging experience makes them a resource for others, too. They know which Italian restaurant, or cognac, or jeweler is the best; they know what new movies are worth seeing and what the latest news and trends are.

Healthy Sevens, however, know that life is most satisfying when they keep their feet on the ground and work within certain constraints. Their enthusiasm and versatility can make them productive and practical, highly creative and prolific, cross-fertilizing their many areas of interest and skills. They can be highly accomplished "Renaissance people," gifted with virtuosic talents and prodigious skills. If they suffer a setback or disappointment, Sevens bounce back with resilience and renewed energy: very little keeps them down for long.

Sevens want to try everything at least twice: once to see what it is like, and the second time to see if they liked it the first time! Of course, Sevens want their experiences to be as much fun and as enjoyable as possible, although, strictly speaking, that is not always essential. What is important to Sevens is being free, having options, and creating more possibilities for their future.

Sevens' minds are restless and filled with ideas and plans for activities to look forward to. They anticipate the future, virtually licking their lips as they foresee the delicious possibilities that await them. But Sevens do not just *think* about the future: they get out there and actually make it happen. They live their dreams by throwing themselves into action and putting their plans in motion. With their energy and enthusiasm, they get things going!

However, as their restlessness increases and they begin to fear missing out on other pleasures and experiences, average Sevens become less discriminate about the experiences they pursue. They begin to lose a sense of priorities and become hyperactive, throwing themselves into constant activity — into endless busyness. They easily feel trapped or deprived, and this makes it difficult to say "no" to themselves or to deny themselves anything. While this might seem like freedom to them, it actually is a kind of prison that makes it increasingly difficult for them to finish projects or to find satisfaction in what they are doing. They begin to believe that freedom is having no restrictions or responsibilities, but this is a false freedom, and it eventually brings them greater unhappiness.

As this occurs, Sevens begin to flee from their inner anxieties by engaging in more distractions and activities. They expect that they and their lives should be exciting and "dazzling" all the time. Increasingly uninhibited, they grab attention and discharge anxiety with storytelling, joking around, exaggeration, and wisecracking. Others may find this behavior amusing and irreverently entertaining for a while, but for most people, even other Sevens, scattered energy eventually becomes tiresome. This only frustrates average Sevens, and unless others are willing to keep up with them, for better or worse, the Seven moves on to greener pastures. Often, this leads to a dissipation of their energy and a loss of focus. While Sevens are often brilliant, once in flight from themselves, they often fail to actualize their many talents or live up to their potential.

In brief, Sevens want to maintain their freedom and happiness, to have a wide variety of interesting, fun experiences and choices, to keep their options open, to avoid missing out on anything worthwhile, to have more pleasure, to keep themselves excited and occupied, and to avoid and discharge pain. *Sevens do not want* to feel trapped or limited by having few choices or options, to be bored or feel guilty, to let their anxieties arise for long, to be slowed down, to be still and quiet for long periods of time, or to dwell in the past.

Their Hidden Side

On the surface, Sevens would like to convince themselves and everyone else that they are always feeling "fabulous" — having the time of their lives. Of course, the truth is often somewhat different. Sevens, like all human beings, are vulnerable to anxiety, depression, loneliness, and other difficult feelings. At times, Sevens sincerely want to tell others how they actually feel, but they often feel compelled to keep spirits high, even if privately they are miserable themselves. Yet, they also struggle with fears of not being taken seriously and a sense that others will misinterpret their positive approach to life as a lack of feeling or depth. In private, Sevens struggle with loneliness, grief, and self-doubt, and are as prone to depression as any other type. Most of all, Sevens fear a gnawing feeling that they will never *really* get what they truly want in life. So they settle for other pleasures that they hope will make them happy enough, or at least pleasantly distracted from the more painful disappointments in their lives.

Relationship Issues

Sevens are often sought out as companions because of their energy, openness to experience, and high spirits. They are like a breath of fresh air to more withdrawn or subdued types and can generally be relied on to be stimulating, engaging, and fun. Sevens can also be generous with themselves and their resources. They feel that good times are best enjoyed when others are enjoying them too, and they want to have someone to share their adventures and discoveries with. But the very high-energy approach that draws people to Sevens can also exhaust their partners. Others can tire of the nonstop stream of activities and plans and want more quiet time with Sevens, which less healthy Sevens may resist. Other relationship problems include these:

- Becoming so involved with expressing their thoughts and ideas that they do not really listen to others.

- Becoming impatient or critical of others' slower pace.
- Getting flighty or seeking distractions when important relationship challenges arise.
- Fearing that others will not support them if they are down or depressed.
- Expecting the partner to provide gratification, entertainment, or support immediately on demand.
- Being unwilling — or very slow — to make commitments.

The Passion: Gluttony

Sevens enjoy life most when they feel stimulated, awake, and refreshed by life's amazing diversity. But to the extent that they are harboring unacknowledged feelings of inner emptiness or loneliness, Sevens become anxious and can get into the habit of seeking constant stimulation as a way of distracting themselves from their anxiety. At such times, they are like starving refugees released at a banquet: they gobble up every experience that is offered to them, often without discriminating the experiences that would be most satisfying. And because their minds are so revved up with options and exciting possibilities, the experiences that they are having hold little possibility for actually getting through to them. Sevens are so much looking forward to the next great experience that the experience they are having *now* cannot satisfy them. Thus, they remain in a state of perpetual hunger — restlessly seeking the magic combination of circumstances that they believe will fulfil them once and for all.

At Their Best

When they are balanced and in their own center, healthy Sevens can harness their enormous enthusiasm and curiosity and still stay focused and deeply engaged with tasks until they are brought to completion. They can set priorities and work within limitations, imposing restrictions on themselves from the recognition that a certain degree of self-restraint actually makes them more productive and much happier. Healthy Sevens can say "no" to themselves without feeling deprived because they are more in touch with their own Inner Guidance and their ability to know what will fulfill them most deeply. From this sense of fulfillment, healthy Sevens move toward others and into the world from a sense of abundance and joy, feeling intensely blessed to be alive and able to enjoy the many enriching experiences that life brings them.

Healthy Sevens are also steady and grounded, able to honor commitments and to take personal responsibility for their actions. In short, they grow up emotionally and move from being "eternal youths" to being mature people, able to look both inward at themselves and outward at life, accepting all that they find in both realms. They become truly "celebratory" and filled with gratitude, resolving their inner hunger and allowing them to feel that they never have to fear that they will be deprived of anything truly worthwhile.

Personality Dynamics and Variations

Under Stress (Seven Goes to Average One)

Sevens value their spontaneity and so tend to follow their impulses, for better or for worse. As a result, they can become scattered in their attention and energy, leaping from one promising idea to the next, from one activity to another. While this can be exciting, it often leaves Sevens frustrated with themselves because they feel that they are not accomplishing as much as they would like to. At such times, they begin to behave like average Ones — pulling in the reins on themselves and trying to get more organized and self-controlled. But because they are trying to *impose* order and control on themselves, they begin to feel trapped and restricted. This only makes them more frustrated, impatient, and irritable. They may, for instance, become critical of their own creative ideas before they have really had a chance to develop them. Similarly, they cannot avoid feeling disappointment with people and many aspects of their environment. Nothing seems to meet their expectations, and they can become harsh and perfectionistically critical with themselves and with others.

Security (Seven Goes to Average Five)

Sevens often feel it is their duty to entertain others and to keep their environment positive and exciting. Over time, this can be exhausting — even for Sevens. When they are tired of being "on" for everyone, they may choose to withdraw even from their intimates and seek seclusion and noninterference. This can come as a shock to others. ("You've been out having fun with everyone else, so why are you so quiet and unavailable with me?") They no longer want to put out energy for anyone else, and can become almost obsessively focused and preoccupied. They can also be surprisingly withdrawn and isolated, like Fives. Their body language and aloof responses let others know that they want space and privacy. At such times, Sevens make no effort to entertain or energize others. Like Fives, they retreat from contact and attempt to restore their energy.

Integration (Seven Goes to Healthy Five)

As Sevens learn to relax and to tolerate their uncomfortable feelings more completely, they stop using their restless minds to distract themselves. Their minds become quiet, clear, and focused, allowing Sevens to tap more deeply into their reserves of creativity and insight. They are able to prioritize not by imposing some arbitrary order on themselves but by following their true interests and staying with them. Thus, they become far more productive, satisfied, and really satisfying as companions. Their capacity to find connections and to synthesize information is not drawn off into tangents — they produce results, and this gives them grounds for real confidence in themselves and in life. As they experience the world more deeply, they find each moment fascinating, profound, and revelatory. The idea of boredom becomes absurd as they savor the incredible mysteries of existence, moment by moment.

The Instincts in Brief

Self-Preservation Sevens: Getting Mine (Ichazo's "Defenders")

Self-Preservation Sevens are the most materialistic Sevens. This does not necessarily mean that they are always accumulating possessions, but they do thoroughly enjoy the things of the material world. They also enjoy *thinking about* acquiring possessions and experiences. Thus, reading catalogues, restaurant guides, movie reviews, travel books, and brochures is often a favorite pastime. Generally, however, they are not daydreamers: they want to actually do or buy the things they are thinking about. Exploring the different pleasures the world offers seems to Self-Pres Sevens what life is about. They love shopping and are especially thrilled by the prospect of getting a great bargain — obtaining the desired object or experience at well below the "normal" cost. Thus, they tend to be the person to consult for a good hotel in a particular city or to find the best place to buy a new laptop computer. Often, they will cultivate friends who are knowledgeable about mutual interests to exchange information about bargains and to stay up with the newest developments. Many Self-Pres Sevens like to "live large" and may spend more than they can afford to sustain their appetite for experience and luxury. Unconsciously, they may have unrealistic expectations that the world should provide them with whatever they need on demand. To the extent that Sevens succumb to this expectation, they are likely to be frustrated and disappointed.

Sexual Sevens: The Neophile (Ichazo's "Suggestibility")

Sexual Sevens seek stimulation, especially the stimulation of whatever is new, cutting edge, or exotic. They are extremely curious and often intellectually avid, and they bring the same searching engagement to their relationships. Sexual Sevens love to meet new people, to learn about them, and to get intensely involved with them — whether through conversation, shared adventures, or sexual experiences. They are often highly charismatic, having no trouble capturing people's attention with their energy, wit, and genuine desire to connect with people. They often frustrate themselves and others, however, because their attention is easily captured by what promises excitement. Sexual Sevens can shift from one intense focus to another too quickly for their own good. They can become easily enthused about a new idea, person, or experience without checking it out thoroughly, often leading to regrets later on, either in business or in relationships. When less healthy, they may indiscriminately pursue relationships or unusual, even dangerous, experiences for the excitement that they bring and to counteract boredom and inner deadness. The search for a variety of exotic and intense experiences can leave them burned out and dissipated.

Social Sevens: Missing Out (Ichazo's "Social Sacrifice")

Social Sevens are highly people-oriented and somewhat idealistic, so they are sometimes mistaken for Twos. They like entertaining and gathering "the gang" for various outings and adventures. They love conversation, launching new projects with others, brainstorming, and initiating creative endeavors. Social Sevens are also looking for a place to invest their idealism — they feel they have much to offer the world but are forever searching for the perfect vehicle through which to express their talents and aspirations. While Social Sevens like being involved with people and activities, because they are Sevens, they also tend to feel that they are losing options when they commit to a particular person or course of action. Thus, they tend to have problems with making a commitment because they want to be involved but feel trapped once they get involved. One way that Social Sevens navigate this conflict is by agreeing to do too many things with too many people. They also tend to make back-up plans regarding agreements. ("If lunch with Sarah falls through, I'll invite Mike too, just to make sure someone's there . . .") Naturally, other are often caught off guard by sudden changes of plans, and, oddly, no one really gets the Social Seven's attention. Social Sevens may also sabotage good relationships while secretly hoping that someone better will come along.

Sevens grow by recognizing that real happiness is available anytime, anywhere: the price of admission is their willingness and ability to be quiet, to be still inside themselves, and to open their eyes to the wonder and richness of life all around them. Once Sevens understand this, they are able to assimilate their experiences in depth. They discover that every moment can make them feel deeply grateful and appreciative — truly awed by the wonders of life. Moreover, their openness and inner quiet brings them a sense of life beyond the physical, a spiritual reality, that begins to shine through the material world. The healthy Seven understands that by being still within, a quiet joy begins to pervade all of life — a deep satisfaction in existence that cannot ever be taken away.

See *Personality Types,* 259–96; *Understanding the Enneagram,* 54–57, 105–12, and 344–46; and *The Wisdom of the Enneagram,* 260–86.

13. Type Eight: The Challenger

The Powerful, Dominating Type:
Self-Confident, Decisive, Willful, and
Confrontational

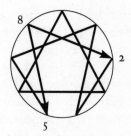

Generally, Eights are strong, assertive, resourceful, independent, determined, action-oriented, pragmatic, competitive, straight-talking, shrewd, and insistent.

Eights get into conflicts by being blunt, willful, domineering, forceful, defiant, confrontational, bad-tempered, rageful, cynical, and vengeful.

At their best, Eights are honorable, heroic, empowering, generous, gentle, constructive, initiating, decisive, and inspiring.

Recognizing Eights

Type Eight exemplifies the desire to be independent and to take care of oneself. Eights are assertive and passionate about life, meeting it head on with self-confidence and strength. They have learned to stand up for themselves and have a resourceful, "can-do" attitude. They are determined to be self-reliant and free to pursue their own destiny. Thus, Eights are natural leaders: honorable, authoritative, and decisive, with a solid, commanding presence. They take initiative and make things happen, protecting and providing for the people in their lives while empowering others to stand on their own. They embody solidity and courage, using their talents and vision to construct a better world for everyone depending on the range of their influence.

Most of all, Eights are people of vision and action. They can take what looks like a useless, broken-down shell of a building and turn it into a beautiful home or office or hospital. Likewise, they see possibilities in people, and they like to offer incentives and challenges to bring out people's strengths. Eights agree with the saying "Give a person a fish and they eat for a day. But teach them how to fish, and they can feed themselves for life." Eights know this is true because they have often taught themselves "how to fish." They are self-starters and enjoy constructive activity — building up themselves, others, and their world.

Eights occasionally take on big challenges to see if they can pull off the impossible or turn a hopeless cause into a great success. But they generally do not do so unless they are fairly sure that the odds are on their side and that they will have the resources to pull off a "long shot" and make it look easy. Others look to them in times of crisis because they know that Eights are willing to make tough decisions and to take the heat if things go wrong.

Honor is also important to Eights because their word is their bond. When they say "You have my word on this," they mean it. Eights want to be *respected*, and healthy Eights also extend respect to others, affirming the dignity of whomever they encounter. They react strongly when they see someone being taken advantage of or treated in a demeaning or degrading manner. They will step in and stop a fight to protect the weak or disadvantaged or to "even the score" for those who they feel have been wronged. Similarly, Eights would not hesitate to give up their seat on the train to an old or sick person, but they would have to be dragged away bodily if anyone tried to make them give it up without their consent.

Nothing much about Eights is half-hearted. They have powerful feelings and drives and often have a major impact on the people around them — for good or for ill. Eights are more intense and direct than most, and they expect others to meet these qualities as well. Indirectness of any kind drives them crazy, and they will keep pushing and raising their energy level until they feel that others have sufficiently responded to them.

Many Eights have some kind of a dream for themselves and their "inner circle," and being the practical-minded people that they are, this often involves money-making projects, business ventures, philanthropy, and the like. They may start and run their own business or set someone up in a situation or simply play the state lottery on a regular basis. Not all Eights have a lot of money, but most are looking for some kind of "big break" that would give them the independence, respect, and sense of power that they typically want. They can also be highly competitive, enjoying the challenges and risks of their own enterprises. They are hard-working and pragmatic — "rugged individualists," and wheeler-dealers who are always thinking of a new angle and constantly have a new project underway.

Less healthy Eights can become extremely controlling, self-important, confrontational, and highly territorial. They may respond to others by swaggering and being willful, bluffing and "throwing their weight around" in various ways. Average Eights are full of bluster and bravado to get people to fall in line with their desires, and if they encounter resistance, they will try to control and dominate people more openly and aggressively. Whether they are running a multinational corporation or a family of two, they want it understood that they are firmly and clearly in charge.

In brief, **Eights want** to be self-reliant, to prove their strength and independence, to be important in their world, to have an impact on their environment, to have the unquestioned loyalty of their inner circle, and to stay in control of their situation. **Eights do not want** to feel weak or vulnerable, to feel out of control, to be dependent on others, to have their decisions or authority questioned, to lose others' backing, or to be surprised by others' unexpected actions.

Their Hidden Side

Eights present a tough, independent image to the world, but under their bravado and layers of armor, there is vulnerability and fear. Eights are affected by the reactions of those closest to them far more than they want to let on. They often expect that others will dislike or reject them, and so they are profoundly touched, even sentimental, when they feel that someone they care about truly understands and loves them. Eights may learn to harden themselves against wanting or expecting tenderness, but they are never entirely successful. No matter how tough, even belligerent, they may become, their desire for nurturance and connection can never be put entirely out of consciousness.

Relationship Issues

Eights are often sought out as partners because they appear so confident, capable, and strong. Others are reassured by their solidity and feel that the Eight will offer protection and stability in the relationship. (When Eights are healthy, this is true.) Eights also exude a great deal of charisma — they have tremendous instinctual energy and many people feel attracted to their intensity. However, other people may be frightened by the same qualities in Eights, and when Eights assert their energy too forcefully, they often create problems in their relationships. Some of their main trouble spots include the following:

- Overreacting to perceived rejection by withdrawing or losing their temper.
- Pushing others to get a more "genuine" response.
- Becoming remote and emotionally unavailable when troubled.
- Becoming possessive and jealous of the partner.
- Seeing the other as an inferior to be shaped and directed; not respecting the partner as an equal.
- Acting out their own psychological issues in rages, binges, or acts of revenge.

The Passion: Lust

Eights want to feel intensely alive: they love the sense of immediacy they get from being engaged with life fully. They do not have much patience with lukewarm responses or half-hearted actions from others. But this desire to be vital and alive can easily deteriorate into a need to constantly *push against* the world — and especially other people. Eights get into the habit of exerting themselves and their influence, increasing the intensity of situations so that they will feel more real and alive. They become like a person aggressively trying to push open a door that opens inwardly. Unfortunately, this approach to life often overwhelms other people who then avoid the Eight, and it can lead to severe stress and even physical breakdown for the Eight herself.

At Their Best

Healthy Eights combine their natural strength and energy with measured, insightful, decision-making and a greater willingness to be emotionally open and available to others. They make loyal friends and will make any sacrifice necessary for the well-being of their loved ones. They feel no need to test their wills against others: they are so secure and grounded in themselves that there is no need to constantly assert themselves, much less control anyone else. Thus, they have greater inner peace themselves and can therefore be enormous sources of support and strength for others. Seeing that they can be a powerful source of blessings in others' lives fills Eights with a deep sense of fulfillment and a kind of benevolent pride in their ability to have a positive impact on the world and on others.

High-functioning Eights are truly heroic, mastering themselves and their passions. They are big-hearted, merciful, and forbearing, carrying others with their strength. Courageous and strong, but also gentle and humble, they are willing to put themselves in jeopardy for the sake of justice and fairness. Very high-functioning Eights have the vision, compassion, and heart to be a tremendous influence for good in the world.

Personality Dynamics and Variations

Under Stress (Eight Goes to Average Five)

Eights usually respond to stress by taking problems and challenges head on. They are bold and assertive in pushing for control and for accomplishing their vision, whatever it might be. But this approach can leave them feeling beleaguered and overwhelmed. When stress levels get too high, Eights may suddenly switch tactics and go into periods of retreat or even isolation, like average Fives. They pull back from the front lines to assess their situation, to strategize, and to see how they can regain control. They may become strangely quiet, secretive, and isolated as they privately explore ways to deal with their problems. Under longer periods of stress, they may also develop a cold, cynical attitude about themselves, other people, and life in general, in the manner of less healthy Fives.

Security (Eight Goes to Average Two)

Eights will sometimes turn toward people they trust to be reassured about the other person's need for them. They have an emotional, even sentimental side that they show only to people with whom they feel safe. They may appear tough and independent in public while privately doting on key people in their lives or, if they lack these, then on their pets. They may also attempt to get intimates to acknowledge their help and support or may want people to depend more completely on them, like average Twos. Hidden feelings of rejection can cause them to seek ways to hold on to those few people they feel close to, including manipulating and undermining the other. Like average Twos, they also become unwilling to acknowledge their real needs or feelings of hurt with people on whom they depend.

Integration (Eight Goes to Healthy Two)

As Eights begin to recognize their powerful emotional armoring and see how much it isolates them unnecessarily, they naturally become more emotionally expressive and generous, like high-functioning Twos. Underneath their drive for self-protection and independence, Eights have big hearts and generous impulses. Once they feel secure enough to let down their guards, they discover how much they care about people and how much they want to support others. In short, they want to be a source of good in the world and to express their love — and at Two they do so. Since they remain Eights, their love is expressed in palpable ways that actually help and support people. It is a love free of sentiment, clinging, or hidden agenda, and through it, Eights find the sense of empowerment and dignity that they have been seeking.

The Instincts in Brief

Self-Preservation Eights: The Survivor (Ichazo's "Satisfactory Survival")

Self-Preservation Eights must live out the Eights' need for independence through the accumulation of power, position, and, sometimes, material wealth. That is not to say that all Self-Pres Eights are wealthy — most are not — but that this variant seeks to have and to control whatever resources they can in order to maintain their independence and dominance. Thus, these Eights make shrewd business people and politicians. They are extremely practical, approaching life with a tough-minded pragmatism they see as being simply "realistic." Often private people, their home is very important to them. Whether man or woman, the Self-Pres Eight rules the roost and is likely to control resources within the household. Positively, they are often excellent providers and have a way of landing on their feet no matter what life throws at them. Trouble spots include difficulty empathizing with the needs of others, especially if they perceive others as weak or ineffectual. Self-Pres Eights most typify the shrewd, pragmatic, wheeler-dealer aspect of this personality type.

Sexual Eights: Taking Charge (Ichazo's "Possessiveness")

Sexual Eights are charismatic and emotionally intense: they seem to "smolder." These Eights seek intensity through relationship, and the ups and downs of their lives are often seen in terms of relationship. The Sexual Eight wants to "imprint" their significant other, to leave their mark. Whether they are dealing with love interests or are engaged in other activities, they enjoy the thrill of intense stimulation and can become addicted to adrenaline rushes. They often adore the people they are in love with, but they can develop problems from thinking of the other as a child that they want to shape and develop. Much of this comes from wanting the partner to be strong enough so that the Sexual Eight can relax and surrender themselves. Thus, they may provoke their loved ones in the effort to test their strength or to build it up. Similarly, they like to be challenged by the other, but this can deteriorate into a struggle for dominance in the relationship. They may resort to arguments or verbal sparring as a way of stimulating intensity in the relationship. Sexual Eights can also feel as though they "own" their intimate partner — that they have a right to satisfaction whenever they need it.

Social Eights: Gusto and Camaraderie (Ichazo's "Friendship")

Social Eights like to "live large," and as the name suggests, engage fully in the world. Friendship and loyalty are top values for them, and they are willing to make great sacrifices for the people and causes they care about. At the same time, they expect that others they have bonded with will be similarly loyal to them. (In this regard, they can resemble Sixes, although their energy is bigger and more direct than that of Sixes.) Often, Social Eights will gather a group of friends around them while unofficially acting as the chairperson of the group — the "king" or "queen." They enjoy conversation about sports, politics, rock music, or the latest events on their favorite soap opera — any subject about which they can boldly state opinions and get into debates. Social Eights enjoy the banter and energy of a disagreement about such matters, and they are often surprised to learn that others can be hurt or overwhelmed by the force of their opinions. At such times, they may try to "tone themselves down," but they usually find this an uncomfortable compromise. More often, they seek out friends who they perceive as strong and independent, people who can take a bit of roughhousing and who will not be overwhelmed by them. Less healthy Social Eights have problems with making promises to people that they cannot always fulfill. Conning others and exaggerating situations can become part of the picture.

Eights grow by recognizing that the world is not a battleground to be approached as a gigantic test of wills. They do not have to see life as a "survival of the fittest," a titanic struggle that they must be constantly engaged in. They grow by recognizing that it is their attempt to defy the world and to force everything to bend to their will that is at the root of their problems. They realize that any *real* strength entails vulnerability and openness. They also learn that allowing more openness enables others to get closer to them and to support them in tangible ways. Eights grow by recognizing that more can be accomplished through cooperation and partnership than they can do by themselves or by constantly struggling to impose their will on others.

See also *Personality Types,* 218–45; *Understanding the Enneagram,* 72–76 and 252–54.

14. Type Nine: The Peacemaker

The Easygoing, Self-Effacing Type:
Receptive, Reassuring, Agreeable, and
Complacent

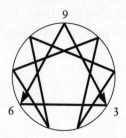

Generally, Nines are patient, steady, easygoing, receptive, relaxed, unself-conscious, agreeable, uncomplicated, contented, comforting, sensual, and idealizing.

Nines get into conflicts by being emotionally unavailable, complacent, unaware of their own anger, ineffectual, inattentive, passive-aggressive, unrealistic, resigned, and stubborn.

At their best, Nines are self-aware, dynamic, proactive, inclusive, steadfast, healing, natural, imaginative, serene, exuberant, engaged, and passionate.

Recognizing Nines

Type Nine exemplifies the desire for wholeness, peace, and harmony in our world. Nines are easygoing, emotionally stable people. They are open and unself-consciously serene, trusting and patient with themselves and others. Their openness allows them to be at ease with life and with the natural world. As a result, others generally find it easy to be in their company. They are genuinely good-natured and refreshingly unpretentious. Because of their peaceful demeanor, Nines have a talent for comforting and reassuring others and are able to exert a calming, healing influence in difficult or tense situations. They make steady, supportive friends who can listen uncritically to others' problems as well as share their good times. In work settings, they can be excellent mediators, able to harmonize groups and bring people together by really healing conflicts.

Nines can also be quite imaginative and creative, and they enjoy expressing themselves in symbolic ways — through music, dance, images, or mythic stories, for instance. They tend to look at things holistically, focusing on the ways in which seemingly unrelated ideas or events are connected and part of a greater whole. Indeed, Nines are drawn to anything that affirms the fundamental oneness of the world. Whether they are working with concepts, diverse groups of people, art forms, or feuding family members, Nines want to bring everything and everyone back to a harmonious unity.

In short, Nines are the eternal optimists, always wanting to believe the best about other people, with hope for the best for themselves. They hope that every story will end with, ". . . and they all lived happily ever after." Healthy Nines will work hard to make things turn out that way. But average Nines will leave it to "luck and a prayer" — and they may be sorely disappointed.

Average Nines focus on keeping their lives pleasant and uncomplicated. They idealize others and live through a handful of primary identifications — usually with their family and close friends. Out of fear of creating conflicts with these people, average Nines hold back their own reactions and opinions and suppress themselves in many other ways. Oddly, Nines can be quite assertive on behalf of others and will work hard for others' benefit, but they can have great difficulty taking actions on their own behalf or even voicing their own real feelings.

To "maintain the peace," Nines tend not to *show* their upsets very much, except indirectly — perhaps by eating, drinking, or watching television too much to escape into a more pleasant and comforting world. They also absorb a lot of tension and neglect — even outright abuse — before showing any kind of emotional response. But when their anger has been held back for too long, Nines can suddenly blow up, seemingly out of the blue. Once they have gotten something out of their system, Nines hope that the storm has blown over and that things will not go back to the way they were before.

Fearing that change (and potential conflict) will threaten their comfort and peace of mind, average Nines become more complacent and disengaged. They entrench themselves in comforting habits and routines, puttering around and finding various kinds of busywork to lose themselves in. But the longer they do this, the more difficulty they have rousing themselves to take decisive action or to assert themselves in any meaningful way. They become passive, walking away from problems and brushing them under the rug. Their thinking becomes hazy and ruminative, mostly daydreaming about happy memories or passing time telling comforting stories. They begin to "tune out" reality to protect themselves from anxiety, often seeming "oblivious" and unresponsive as a result. Average Nines use passive-aggressive acts and stubbornness to resist attempts to engage them. But their peace of mind is little more than an avoidance of problems — a clinging to fantasies and unrealistic hopes.

Low-functioning Nines can become fatalistic and resigned, trudging through life as if nothing can be done to improve their situation. Engaged in wishful thinking, looking for easy, magical solutions, Nines keep "waiting for their ship to come in," but without some constructive effort on their part, they may wait a long time, indeed.

In brief, Nines want to find unity and wholeness, to create harmony in their environment, to feel spacious and at ease, to emphasize the positive, to avoid conflicts and tension, to resist change and preserve things as they are, and to ignore whatever would upset or disturb them. *Nines do not want* to have conflicts with loved ones, to feel cut off or separated from others, to be angry, to be upset or disturbed, to have their habits or routines interrupted, to be emotionally uncomfortable, or to be forced to face unpleasant realities.

Their Hidden Side

On the surface, Nines appear to be the most easygoing, pleasant people imaginable. They go along with others' wishes, apparently without any desire other than to make sure everyone is at ease and happy. But their hidden side is that they often suppress a huge well of anger that they conceal even from themselves. Nines want to get along with others, but they also want to hold on to their independence and autonomy — they do not want to be "messed with." To the extent that they feel they cannot do the latter without endangering their connections with the important people in their lives, they become resentful and enraged — although they also feel that they can never let this anger out without destroying their relationships. Thus, for Nines to develop themselves and their potential, they must come to grips with their suppressed rage and find constructive outlets for this energy.

Relationship Issues

People are often drawn to Nines as potential life partners for many reasons. They are comforting and supportive, warm and sensual. They adapt well to domestic life and enjoy being with their partner. And they *seem* to be utterly without any significant needs of their own. They are uncomplicated and undemanding to the extent that others get the false notion that the Nine will meet their needs without needing anything much from them. Therein lies the source of problems with Nines in relationship. Of course, Nines do have personal needs, but to the extent that they are not being met, Nines shut down and withdraw from the other rather than risk getting into a conflict. Key issues include these:

- Going along with others or agreeing to things the Nine has no intention of complying with.
- Becoming emotionally unavailable to others: disengaging their attention or withdrawing rather than dealing with issues.
- Wanting to feel close with someone while asserting independence in their behavior.
- The "No Talk Rule" — refusing to discuss the real problems.
- Suppression, control, and outbursts of temper — all of which are generally unrecognized and unacknowledged by the Nine.
- Emotional "collapsing" as a way of stopping discussion about troubling topics.

The Passion: Sloth

Nines pay a price for their easygoing demeanor because much of it depends on their staying out of contact with their instinctual energies. Nines do this for two reasons. First, much of their instinctual aliveness is used to suppress their anger and frustration with people and with themselves. To experience their anger directly is extremely threatening to Nines: they feel that their rage could destroy their peaceful world very quickly. In order to stay in their unrealistic, idealized world, they must constantly suppress their anger and instincts over and over again. But when Nines attempt to dam those energies, the result is inner numbness and general fatigue because so much of their inner resources is devoted to keeping their anger and instincts at bay.

Thus, Nines end up becoming passive and disengaged. Rousing themselves to take an active role in their lives seems difficult — it will all be "too much trouble" becomes a constant refrain. So they retreat into safe and comforting routines — and the passion of sloth. Understood this way, sloth is not necessarily physical laziness; rather, it is an inner disengagement, a reluctance to show up in one's life with all of one's passion, immediacy, and presence available. The longer Nines remain in the state of sloth, the more they become convinced that they can never do what it takes to engage fully in their lives.

At Their Best

As Nines learn to assert themselves more freely, they experience greater peace, equanimity and contentment. Their self-possession enables them to have a profound effect on the world because they are truly present to themselves. They are intensely alive, awake, exuberant, and alert. They have learned not to give up their power to others or withhold themselves from a fear of self-assertion. They become dynamic and joyful, actively working for peace and healing their world as a result. They have enormous dignity and a genuine serenity that comes from deeply accepting the human condition.

Thus, high-functioning Nines are extraordinarily vital, self-possessed, and independent. They understand that by being grounded in the present moment, they can have both independence and connection with others: it is not an either/or situation. Further, their natural creativity and leadership can come to the fore because they are in touch with their own strength and capacities. People also instinctively trust healthy Nines because they will use their active influence to do what is necessary to create and sustain a truly harmonious environment, one in which everyone can thrive.

Personality Dynamics and Variations

Under Stress (Nine Goes to Average Six)

Nines attempt to avoid anxiety and conflict by detaching emotionally from active participation and by not talking about their real concerns and issues. But they can only use this defense up to a point, beyond which they can no longer contain their anxiety, frustration, and fear. At such times, they will begin to exhibit many of the characteristics and behaviors of average-to-unhealthy Sixes. The usually stable, easygoing Nine becomes worried, testy, and defensive. They begin to see others as the source of their unease, complaining to anyone who will listen, and blaming everyone else for their distress. They may also have issues with authority, feeling put upon or controlled by those they see as having power over them. Under prolonged stress, Nines completely lose their placid demeanor and become more and more reactive and nervous. They may seek help and reassurance from others but may just as quickly disparage them for "dominating" or "overwhelming" them.

Security (Nine Goes to Average Three)

Nines usually feel unimportant and may feel that their own needs and viewpoints are not worth mentioning. With trusted others, however, they may attempt to demonstrate their value, desirability, or even superiority, in the manner of average Threes. In secure situations, Nines will deal with stress also by working more and being productive — even if their productivity is really "busy-work" designed to keep awareness of more crucial problems out of awareness. This busyness is the Nine's way of trying to build a sense of confidence and value. Nines may also try to impress intimates with their accomplishments, status, or attractiveness — although, ironically, they are usually completely unaware of how they are coming across to others.

Integration (Nine Goes to Healthy Three)

As Nines work through their belief that they are unimportant, they begin to recognize their true value. They see that others really do want them to show up and share themselves fully. Healthy Nines begin to understand that their very existence makes them valuable — God did not make a mistake in creating them. Their experience is much like the adventures of the Jimmy Stewart character in *It's a Wonderful Life*. They see that the world would be poorer without them and that they have much to contribute to their fellow human beings. They understand that the peace of mind they seek comes from fully sharing their talents, intelligence, and heart with the world. Thus, integrating Nines begin to invest time and energy in themselves, to develop their talents, and to feel a healthy degree of self-esteem. In short, they learn to take pleasure in their own value and goodness.

The Instincts in Brief

Self-Preservation Nines: The Comfort Seeker (Ichazo's "Appetite")

Self-Pres Nines are perhaps the most easygoing Nines, but they are also the most likely to need time alone, untroubled by other people's influence and requirements. They seek a sense of well-being through comfort: familiar routines, "comfort foods," and a supportive, uncomplicated environment are all highly valued. Self-Pres Nines have their own way of doing things, their own pace, and their own philosophy of life, and they will stubbornly resist any effort to change any of these things. Self-Pres Nines are also people of few words, preferring to communicate in nonverbal ways. They often pretend to be less savvy and aware than they actually are, as if tempting other people to underestimate them — so that they will be left alone. Positively, they are grounded and patient, possessing a great deal of common sense. They tend to have problems with overindulging themselves in food and drink, or conversely with rigorously controlling their diets — this is especially true of Self-Pres Nines with the One wing. They may also lack physical exercise. In any case, having their routine and lifestyle change is very challenging for them.

Sexual Nines: Merging (Ichazo's "Union")

Sexual Nines seek a sense of well-being by finding something or someone to merge with. They want to be at one with the world, with beauty, with nature, but especially with a special, ideal lover. That being said, Sexual Nines have many anxieties about losing themselves by submerging their identity in the other. Thus, they can sometimes appear ambivalent and emotionally conflicted, like Fours or Sixes. They sometimes attempt to "solve" the inner conflict between their desire for merging and their desire for independence by "triangulation." They engage in two separate, simultaneous relationships that serve different needs while never completely showing up in either. Needless to say, this can create the kinds of conflicts that Nines are trying to avoid.

The overall affect of Sexual Nines is one of gentleness, ease, and flow, and they seek these qualities in others and in the environment. They also tend to be highly sensual, enjoying tastes, textures, and sensations. Although they resemble Fours in this regard, being ethereal and dreamy, their sensuality is earthy and embodied and they are not as self-aware or self-doubting as Fours. Sexual Nines tend to be more imaginative than the other variants — often with elements of gentle whimsy and heroic fantasy. They see the world in magical terms, investing even ordinary objects with a warm glow. They seem to take in the world with a wide-eyed wonder and have a characteristic childlike aura about them.

Social Nines: One Happy Family (Ichazo's "Participation")

Social Nines seek a sense of well-being through social connection and friendship. People of this variant may often not seem like Nines because they are usually more outgoing, active, and involved in their world. These Nines express more warmth and affection. They tend to be idealistic and are often supportive of causes, acting as the "social glue" in many organizations and groups. But even in the midst of social activity, Social Nines remain strangely unaware of and unaffected by the problems of others. They are drawn to situations in which they feel they can belong, but they also internally hold themselves apart — usually by emotionally distancing themselves from others while maintaining an outward friendliness.

Since social Nines tend to be affable and cheerful and enjoy having different experiences, they can resemble Sevens. They also tend to be more task-oriented: they enjoy working on projects and being involved in meaningful activities with others, so they can also resemble Threes. Unlike Threes, however, Social Nines have difficulty sustaining efforts on their own behalf. They do not easily pursue their own goals and tend to get sidetracked by social interactions and others' needs and agendas.

Nines grow by recognizing that the more they seek peace of mind by turning away from conflicts and problems, the greater is the likelihood that they will bring about disturbances in their lives and relationships. Their avoidance of conflicts causes others to *have* conflicts with them. Growing Nines must also remember that they will never have union with anyone else unless and until they have union with themselves. If they are accommodating to a fault, they will eventually lose the other person because they have never possessed themselves. When they learn that self-assertion is not an aggressive act but a positive thing, Nines are in a position to truly bring peace and harmony to everyone in their environment.

See *Personality Types,* 338–75; *Understanding the Enneagram* 60–62, 119–26, and 349–51; and *The Wisdom of the Enneagram,* 314–40.

PART THREE

15. Interpretation: Getting More out of the RHETI

Although discovering your basic personality type is the primary object of the RHETI, you can also gain more information about your personality and its dynamics from it.

In most cases, the highest score is your basic personality type; however, occasionally the basic type may be only two or three points higher than another type, or several types may be equal. There may also be other unusual results. This section is concerned with interpreting the RHETI, particularly in cases in which the results are somewhat ambiguous.

In this chapter, we will also discuss the nine personality types as psychological Functions operating within each of us and will briefly comment on patterns and issues frequently seen with this questionnaire.

The Functions

From one point of view, each of the personality types is a metaphor for a wide range of behavior and attitudes, just as in astrology different "houses" denote particular areas of human activity. The nine personality types of the Enneagram can thus be regarded as psychological "functions" and groups of potentials for a wide spectrum of healthy to unhealthy traits. One reason we are all similar is that all nine Functions operate in each of us; one reason we are different is that their proportion and balance within our psyches is different.

We have given two names to each Function because each personality type represents two major areas of activity — a Function that characterizes an internally held *attitude* of the type, and a second Function that characterizes the type's observable *behavior*. High scores in one or more of the types indicate that you have already developed these Functions (that is, the capacities of these types), whereas relatively low scores indicate that you need to give more attention to developing these potentials. (The following short sketches of the Functions are suggestive, rather than exhaustive, treatments of this aspect of the Enneagram. For more qualities associated with each type as a Function, read the descriptions provided in *Personality Types* and *Understanding the Enneagram* with this interpretation in mind.)

Understood as a series of interrelated psychological Functions, the nine personality types of the Enneagram reveal the full range of one's personality. The balance of the Functions in each person produces that person's distinctive "fingerprint" or "signature": while the basic type remains constant as the dominant aspect of the personality, the other Functions in the overall pattern change over time.

Looked at from the viewpoint of the Functions, our basic personality type can thus be seen for what it is — a dominant Function around which we have organized our central response to reality — while the other eight types represent the wide range of potentials that exist within us.

The Instinctive Triad

TYPE EIGHT. The Functions of *Self-Assertion* and *Leadership:* The potential for self-confidence, self-determination, self-reliance, magnanimity, and the ability to take personal initiative. Negatively, the potential for the domination of others, crude insensitivity, combativeness, and ruthlessness.

TYPE NINE. The Functions of *Receptivity* and *Interpersonal Mediation:* The potential for emotional stability, acceptance, unselfconsciousness, emotional and physical endurance, and creating harmony with others. Negatively, the potential for passivity, disengaged emotions and attention, neglectfulness, and dissociation.

TYPE ONE. The Functions of *Rationality* and *Social Responsi-*

bility: The potential for moderation, conscience, maturity, self-discipline, and delayed gratification. Negatively, the potential for rigid self-control, impersonal perfectionism, judgmentalism, and self-righteousness.

The Feeling Triad

TYPE TWO. The Functions of *Empathy* and *Altruism:* the potential for other-directedness, thoughtfulness for others, necessary self-sacrifice, generosity, and nurturance. Negatively, the potential for intrusiveness, possessiveness, manipulation, and self-deception.

TYPE THREE. The Functions of *Self-Esteem* and *Self-Development.* The potential for ambition, self-improvement, personal excellence, self-assurance, and social distinction. Negatively, the potential for pragmatic calculation, arrogant narcissism, the exploitation of others, and hostility.

TYPE FOUR. Functions of *Self-Awareness* and *Artistic Creativity:* The potential for intuition, sensitivity, individualism, self-expression, and self-revelation. Negatively, the potential for self-consciousness, self-absorption, self-doubt, self-indulgence, and depression.

The Thinking Triad

TYPE FIVE. The Functions of *Abstract Understanding* and *Expert Knowledge:* The potential for curiosity, perceptiveness, the acquisition of knowledge, inventive originality, and technical expertise. Negatively, the potential for speculative theorizing, emotional detachment, eccentricity, social isolation, and mental distortions.

TYPE SIX. The Functions of *Trust* and *Social Affiliation:* The potential for emotional bonding with others, group identification, sociability, industriousness, loyalty, and commitment to larger efforts. Negatively, the potential for dependency, ambivalence, divisiveness, rebelliousness, anxiety, and inferiority feelings.

TYPE SEVEN. The Functions of *Responsiveness* and *Enjoy-*

ment: The potential for enthusiasm, productivity, achievement, skill acquisition, curiosity, breadth, and the desire for change and variety. Negatively, the potential for hyperactivity, superficiality, impulsiveness, excessiveness, and escapism.

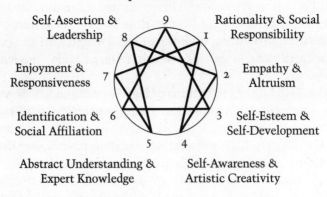

The Enneagram of the Functions

Patterns and Issues

The Construction of the RHETI

Naturally, we hope that this new validated version of the RHETI will be more accurate, more useful in self-help and therapeutic situations, more evocative, and easier to take.

Approximately twenty-five of the questions in version 2.0 have been changed or replaced in version 2.5. After extensive testing and analysis, we replaced questions that were proving less accurate than others as we obtained a larger sample size. Sometimes, we replaced a statement because we recognized ambiguities in it that could lead to interpretations other than the ones we intended.

Furthermore, all of the statements in version 2.5 of the RHETI have been put in the *past* tense to remind people to take the test from that point of view. Since people are instructed to take the RHETI "as they have been most of their lives," it seemed helpful to have the statements reflect this past-orientation. (After taking the RHETI from the point of view of the past, you may wish to take it "as you are now," in the present; when you do so, however, you will, of course, have to remind yourself to answer the past-tense questions as if they were in the present.)

Insights we received from those attending our workshops and Trainings revealed new dimensions of the types that are extremely subtle and complex, and we are constantly uncovering new aspects of them. Over time, we also learned how to best work with the "forced choice" format itself, drafting pairs of statements in which people could more clearly discern which of the two statements was more true of them.

When we realized the multiple parameters in which we had to operate, the conceptual constraints mounted quickly:

- The statements must specify something people can recognize in themselves while avoiding statements that are too abstract or so subtle that only a person in analysis would be aware of them.
- The statements must not describe attitudes that are either too healthy or too unhealthy, particularly the latter, since experience indicated that people did not respond honestly to anything that would reflect too negatively on them.
- There must be no sex bias to the statements.
- Ideally, the statements should not simply negate each other ("I like ice cream" versus "I don't like ice cream").
- Preferably, the statements should avoid "Enneagram jargon" and other language that would alert readers to which type was being tested.
- The statements must all discriminate to a level of 70 percent or better between the two types being tested, and the seven remaining types must split relatively evenly, with four types agreeing with one statement and three agreeing with the other.

- Both statements must reflect attitudes or behaviors at the same Level of Development for their respective types so that one statement does not seem to be healthier and therefore more attractive than the alternative.

Several other parameters also had to be kept in mind as we drafted statements for the test. Needless to say, this has been a time-consuming and arduous task, but we feel that this new version is a significant advance that will help the entire field go forward.

Fluctuating Scores

If you take the RHETI several times, your basic type should remain the same, although you will probably find that the scores for the other types will rise or fall depending on other influences in your life. Someone having problems with a significant relationship, for instance, is likely to register higher or lower scores in types associated with concerns about relationships, such as Two, Four, and Six. Someone who has been putting a lot of time and energy into work or is having career problems is likely to produce elevated scores in types One, Three, and Eight. After the troubled relationship or the career issues have been resolved (one way or another), the profile for that person may change yet again. The scores for the person's basic personality type may also be affected, although it will generally remain the high score (or at least one of the top three scores).

Wings

Your (dominant) wing may be indicated by the higher score of one of the types on either side of your basic type. For example, if you test as a Two, your wing will be One or Three, whichever has the higher score.

The second highest *overall* score on the RHETI is not necessarily that of the wing. For instance, a Six's second highest score may be Nine; this does not mean that his or her wing is Nine. (Look at the scores for Five and Seven; the higher is likely the Six's wing.)

In all cases, the proportion of the wing to that of the basic type must be taken into consideration. Some people will have a relatively high wing score in proportion to their basic type. Some will have a moderate or even a low proportion of wing to basic type. This consideration is significant in understanding a person's reactions and behavior, particularly if a prediction of his or her performance is being attempted, as in a business setting. (For a longer explanation of the proportion of wing to basic type, see *Personality Types*, 418–21.)

In some cases, the "wrong" wing will score higher than the person's actual wing (as determined by subjects themselves or by trained Enneagram judges). An anomaly such as this could result when the qualities of the basic type and the wing are in conflict. In the descriptions of the wings in *Personality Types*, we noted that some combinations of the basic type and wing reinforce each other while other combinations are in conflict. For example, many qualities of the Four and the Three are in opposition, whereas the qualities of the Four and the Five reinforce each other; this situation exists for all the types and their associated wings.

You may also get a high score in a wing other than the one you are expecting because of current factors in your life. For example, someone who had been typed both by himself and by three trained Enneagram teachers as a Seven with a Six-wing tested as a Seven with an Eight-wing. In this instance, although the RHETI correctly diagnosed the subject's basic type, the wing differed from what was expected. A reasonable interpretation is that the subject is in a high-pressure, competitive field where self-confidence and initiative are crucial to success. The subject has been taking more control of his career and has been making a conscious effort to be more assertive. This, coupled with the fact that types Seven and Six are in conflict, possibly caused the subject to register more responses for the Eight than for the Six.

When assessing your wing, it is always a good idea to evaluate the test results by reading the descriptions of both wings in *Personality Types* and deciding which fits you best.

Close Calls

Occasionally, someone's results will be an almost even distribution of scores among the nine types. Of course, the highest score will usually indicate the basic personality type. However, in some rare instances, there may be a tie for the high score, and it will therefore be difficult to draw conclusions about the basic type from the evidence of the test alone. Alternatively, while one score may be higher than the others, the scores for several types may be so close that it is difficult to find easily recognizable patterns among them. For example, in an actual case, a subject scored 19 points — his highest score — in three types, and 18 points in two others.

There are two explanations for this kind of close pattern. First, the subject may have been engaged in therapy or spiritual development for many years and may have resolved the problems and conflicts of his or her personality. (Remember that as essence is developed, personality loses its grip; hence, the more work a person does on himself or herself, the more it eventually becomes difficult to test personality, and scores would be expected to equalize.) It should be noted, however, that very few individuals seem to have attained this degree of integration and nonidentification with their ego. This explanation should therefore be applied rarely and with great caution.

The second explanation for a relatively close distribution of scores is that the subject may *not* have spent much time in personal development and may therefore lack the self-knowledge necessary to take the RHETI properly. (Ironically, this explanation is a reverse of the first.) In this situation, the same pattern results from the subject's identification with too many traits indiscriminately. If this should occur, the subject's personality type may be found by having someone who knows him or her well take the RHETI either with the person or in the person's place. A subject who has obtained the same score in several types should also carefully read the type chapters in this book, and the descriptions in *Personality Types* and *Understanding the Enneagram*, with particular attention to the types' motivations, and then retake the test.

The personality type that most frequently encounters this difficulty is type Nine. Nines have problems seeing themselves because their sense of self is relatively undefined. They have developed their capacity to be unself-conscious and receptive to others; therefore, they tend to see themselves in all of the types and in none very strongly (although there is a tendency for female Nines to misidentify themselves as Twos and for male Nines to misidentify themselves as Fives; see *Understanding the Enneagram*, 214–6 and 233–6). For this reason, they typically have relatively "flat" or evenly distributed scores in the RHETI for all nine types, with Nine among the top two or three scores. Furthermore, since Nines also tend to identify strongly with others, they may mistakenly apply the personality traits of loved ones to themselves. For example, Nines married to Fours may register high scores in Four because of their identification with the Four spouse, not necessarily because they have actually developed the qualities of a Four themselves.

Nines are not the only type to misidentify themselves, however. Because of a strongly held self-image, emotional needs, or social fears, individuals of other types may have extreme difficulty seeing themselves accurately and therefore may produce unexpected (even incorrect) test results. A Three, for example, may test almost equally high or higher in another type because he has come to believe that he must be a particular way to be valued. Threes are unconsciously driven to become whatever was most valued in their family of origin. Thus, Threes from families who valued business acumen and entrepreneurial skills may test high in Eight. Threes from families where intellectual achievement was paramount may test high in Five, and families that value artistic expression would likely produce Threes who would test high in Four.

Sixes tend to misidentify themselves with the RHETI through sheer nervousness and second-guessing themselves. Sixes like to play "devil's advocate" and can always come up with an incident that causes them to doubt what is clearly truer of them. ("Most of my life I have preferred rock and roll to opera, but one time I went to an opera and it was great, so maybe if I listened to more operas I would realize that really . . .") It is therefore important to read the full descriptions of each type and to understand the person's underlying motivations and attitudes to make an accurate assessment.

Beyond this, it is worth noting that while some people may identify their type correctly, they may not want to admit aspects of themselves either to themselves or to anyone else. Obviously, no test of personality can work unless subjects are willing and able to look at themselves honestly and objectively.

Other High Scores

The RHETI does not purport to measure extreme health or unhealth, self-actualization or pathology. The primary concern of this test is to determine your basic personality type, and any other conclusions drawn from the test are relatively speculative.

Furthermore, the statements for each type have been designed to fall within the *healthy-to-average* range of the Levels of Development, that is, between Levels 3 to 6 on the Continuum (see Chapter 5). It would therefore be virtually impossible for pathology to be discovered by this test. High scores in a type in your Direction of Stress (or "Disintegration") may, however, indicate the presence of significant sources of stress in your life at the time of taking the test. While this could alert you to be more aware of possible pressures in your life, *having a high score in the Direction of Stress does not necessarily indicate unhealthy tendencies.* Remember that if the type in your Direction of Stress is understood as a psychological Function, the type is part of your overall personality. All types, no matter how high or low they score on this test, must be taken into consideration.

You can extract more information from the RHETI by adding your scores in several other significant groups: first, according to Triad, which indicates whether your assets and liabilities occur in your *thinking center* (The Thinking Triad — Types Five, Six, and Seven), *feeling center* (The Feeling Triad — Types Two, Three, and Four), or *instinctual center* (The Instinctive Triad — Types Eight, Nine, and One).

A second, and usually more useful, way to analyze your scores is to add them according to what we call the "Hornevian Groups." In *Personality Types* we noted that the psychiatrist Karen Horney's aggressive types, or those who "move against people," correspond to the Enneagram assertive types Three, Seven, and Eight. Her compliant types, or those who "move toward people," correspond to the Enneagram dutiful types One, Two, and Six; and her withdrawn types, or those who "move away from people," correspond to withdrawn types Four, Five, and Nine.

You can use the second two score sheets to add your scores for the withdrawn types (Four, Five, and Nine), your scores for the dutiful types (One, Two, and Six), and your scores for the assertive types (Three, Seven, and Eight) to see the group in which you are highest.

This may help you to analyze scores in ambiguous cases, such as the example of a man who was clearly an Eight (according to an experienced Enneagram teacher) but who tested highest as a One, with Eight coming in a very close second. However, by adding the scores of his three assertive types (Three, Seven, and Eight) it was clear that he was one of the assertive types and most likely an Eight after all. Moreover, the Seven was his third-highest score, which is consistent with his being an Eight with a Seven-wing. Once he heard the description of the Eight during the workshop, he agreed that this was his type, and the correct diagnosis was possible. In another case, a person who had mistyped himself as a Five also had very high scores in the assertive types, and further interviewing and introspection indicated that the person was in fact a Three and not a Five. His low scores in the withdrawn group also indirectly confirmed this analysis.

Please note a special caveat. If you are a woman age thirty or older, and especially if you are from a background in which women were taught to fulfill the role of the caretaker, it is best to question any high type Two scores you may get with the RHETI. While we believe that version 2.5 has fewer instances of false-Two scores, it is not foolproof in this regard. Therefore, if you are a woman and have come out with Two as your highest score, look at the next highest score to see if that type describes you better. For example, a woman at a workshop tested as a Two (24 points) and next as a Six (23 points). After hearing the description of the Six, she realized that it fit her completely and that she was not a Two. Another woman tested as a Two (28 points) and as a Nine (26 points); she turned out to be a Nine who was taught to play the role of the nurturing mother, a role she completely fulfilled. In a sense, she is a Nine playing the role of a Two, as her life history and personal sharing indicated.

Thus, the RHETI is sometimes more correct than our preconceptions and expectations. For example, a person who thinks she is a Four may well test as a Six because she really is a Six. People who are either new to the Enneagram or who have been confused by different interpretations of it often misidentify themselves, and when the RHETI produces a result other than the one they expect, they usually think that the RHETI is wrong.

Unfortunately, the only way to resolve the problem of "which diagnosis is correct?" is for the person to keep an open mind, to go over the RHETI with someone who knows them well, and to carefully read the descriptions of the types in question. In time, the accurate type will probably become clear, and then you will be able to use this knowledge in your psychospiritual practice.

Naturally, even this new version of the RHETI is not perfect. Like all the work being done on the Enneagram, it is a work in progress. While based on an ancient symbol, the application of the Enneagram to psychology is modern, and our understanding of it as a model for human nature is constantly deepening and evolving. Just as there is no ancient "oral tradition" source for the teachings and materials from which Enneagram authors can draw material, so too there is no definitive source to which we can turn for insight. The usefulness and brilliance of the Enneagram lies simply in the fact that it "cleaves the diamond of the psyche along its proper internal lines." It is an extraordinary map that illuminates our way as we discover more about a mysterious reality: human nature — ever the same, ever new.

16. The Universal Enneagram:

Applications in the Real World

This chapter suggests some of the main practical ways in which the Enneagram can be applied in the real world and offers a few simple guidelines and illustrations for each application. These discussions necessarily have to be little more than "the hint of a suggestion" — a sketch for a primer rather than a complete presentation. Even so, it is exciting to see the wide diversity of possible uses of the Enneagram and to realize that much creative work is yet to be done with it. We hope that our own books of Enneagram applications will follow in due time, although there will always remain areas for others to write about, enriching our understanding of the Enneagram and of human nature.

So many practical applications are possible with the Enneagram because it is a framework that clarifies the mutually sustaining, self-balancing components that are part of any complex process. Whenever we wish to understand any process more clearly (and why any course of action does or does not work), we can use the Enneagram as a guide. For example, to start and operate a successful enterprise, one needs vision and confidence (Eight), the ability to bring people together and to listen to them (Nine), ethical standards and quality control (One), the ability to serve people and anticipate their needs (Two), promotional and communication skills (Three), a well-designed product and a sensitivity to its emotional impact on individuals (Four), technical expertise and innovative ideas (Five), teamwork and self-regulating feedback (Six), and energy and optimism (Seven). Thus, each type, *seen metaphorically*, is a necessary component of the whole, and without it something important will be deficient or even entirely missing. This kind of analysis can be made on many different conceptual levels for an amazing variety of phenomena.

We can use the Enneagram to understand a multitude of business applications, relationships, parenting, cultural differences, and personal growth (the main topics in this chapter). We can also use the Enneagram to gain more insight into academic psychology, philosophy, education, biography, the arts (and the styles of composers and creative artists), mythology and the study of archetypes, religion and mysticism, prayer and ascetic practices, spirituality and spiritual direction, psychological testing, brain chemistry, advertising, sales, marketing, and all forms of communication, various kinds of therapy (and the personalities of the psychologists who created them), marriage, career and legal counseling, sports coaching, lawyer and jury selection, politics (and the character of officeholders and those running for office), and various dimensions of cultural studies. These are just some of the areas in which people are either currently applying the Enneagram or seeking more information about how to do so.

No matter how we use the Enneagram, we need first and foremost to discover our own personality type and (where possible) to ascertain the types of those we are dealing with. If the Enneagram is to be used for personal growth, relationships, therapy, or in the business world, one's primary personality type (and those of others) must be accurately assessed. The *Riso-Hudson Enneagram Type Indicator* (version 2.5) provides a reliable, scientifically validated tool for that purpose. But we must remember that discovering our type is only the first step in the process of self-discovery and working with this system. Finding our type is not the final goal but merely the starting place for one of the most fascinating and rewarding journeys of our life.

In Business

Organizations around the world are demanding more accurate information about the needs of clients and employees — and how best to communicate with them. Many are also interested in developing a more humane and person-centered approach to the workplace so that they can attract and retain valuable employees and achieve peak productivity. If we want to maximize our productivity in the workplace, we need to learn *how to manage ourselves* and *how to manage different types of people.* The Enneagram is uniquely suited to meet these needs — and many more — in the business world.

The key to success in any venture is the ability to communicate with others, to inspire them to share your vision and goals, and to provide clear direction and keep things on track through clear feedback. Yet communication is often difficult if personality type is not taken into account, because people tend to believe that others think the same way they do and that others have the same motivations, values, priorities, and reactions as they do.

Even if we understand that different people need to be managed differently, without an adequate idea of *what those differences actually are,* it is difficult to manage people more effectively. Once type differences are taken into account, however, solutions grow out of insights about the nature of each type, its habitual reactions, and its motivations. When type is taken into account, communication becomes exponentially more effective and people can recognize and make the most of *human diversity.* The Enneagram helps managers and personnel at every level understand that there are nine different points of view, nine distinct sets of values, nine different communication styles, nine ways of solving problems — and so forth — and that they are all equally useful and valid. All of the types have something necessary to contribute to a thriving, balanced work environment.

By understanding personality types, we can speak the language of others, which may be very different from our own. Real communication is then possible, and we are able to deal more evenhandedly with conflicts, ineffective work habits, office politics, and different management styles, among other important work issues. The Enneagram lubricates all interactions in the workplace by giving people a common vocabulary and frame of reference. Moreover, it helps retain valuable employees by increasing job satisfaction and productivity. It can be used in an executive search to find the right person for the job — and in executive coaching to help people work at the highest level of their capacities. The Enneagram is also particularly valuable for team development, conflict resolution, negotiation, and leadership development.

Furthermore, the Enneagram helps us see our *own* personality dynamics more clearly. Once we are aware of the importance of personality types, we see that our own style will not be equally effective with everyone. Thus, one of the most useful lessons of the Enneagram is how to move from a management style in which others are expected to mold themselves to our way of thinking and values to a more flexible management style in which we act from an awareness of the strengths and potential contributions of others. By doing so, we help others become more effective themselves — and as a result, harmony, productivity, and satisfaction are likely to increase.

The following brief descriptions of the nine types that we have seen in this book emphasize how they appear in the business world. (We also use different names for some of the types, since in our experience these are more acceptable in the business world.) You may be able to identify yourself or someone else through this brief "paragraph test," and you can use the descriptions to corroborate what you have found by taking the full RHETI in this book or online (at www.EnneagramInstitute.com). Needless to say, these brief descriptions are by no means complete — but they are a good place to see the utility of the Enneagram in this context.

The Nine Types in Business

| Type One
The Reformer | The rational, orderly type. Principled, purposeful, self-controlled, and perfectionistic. Ones are concerned with maintaining quality and high standards. They focus on details and like to improve and streamline procedures. They are often good at coaching others on how to improve themselves, be more efficient, and do things correctly. Well-organized and orderly, they can also be overly critical of themselves and others. They dislike waste and |

sloppiness, but can deteriorate into micro-management and constant, demoralizing criticism. At their best, they have good judgment, make wise decisions, and model ethical and responsible behavior.

Type Two
The Mentor

The helpful, interpersonal type. Generous, appreciative, people-pleasing, and possessive. Twos are sensitive to the needs of others and seek to be of service. They appreciate the talents of others and act as confidants and guides, good at networking people and services. Warm and personable, they are often highly effective at sales and recruiting. However, they typically have trouble saying no to requests and tend to become stressed by trying to help others too much. They dislike impersonal rules and work situations and can deteriorate into favoritism and time-wasting personal over-involvements. At their best, they are empathetic and generous and help build team interpersonal connections.

Type Three
The Achiever

The adaptable, ambitious type. Focused, excelling, driven, and image-conscious. Threes know how to work efficiently to get the job done according to customer expectations. Often attractive, charming, and energetic, they are conscious of the image they project of themselves as well as of their team and company. They like getting recognition and are attracted to success and positions of prestige. They can be competitive and workaholic, driven by the need for status and personal advancement, deteriorating into cutting corners to stay ahead. At their best, they are accomplished and admirable, often seen as inspiring role models by others.

Type Four
The Designer

The introspective, artistic type. Expressive, dramatic, self-absorbed, and temperamental. Fours deliver personalized service and/or develop distinctive products known for their refinement and sense of style. They can be uncompromising in their pursuit of the right effect, word, or design and of gauging the personal impact of a product. They dislike tasks that they feel are not creative or give them room for their personal imprint. They may be hypersensitive to criticism and can deteriorate into moodiness and erratic work habits. At their best, they bring intuition and creativity into the workplace and enrich it with their sense of depth, style, and appreciation of the personal dimension.

Type Five **The Investigator**	The perceptive, provocative type. Curious, innovative, secretive, and eccentric. Fives are tireless learners and experimenters, especially in specialized or technical matters. They like to understand in detail, spend time on research, and follow their curiosity wherever it leads. They are highly analytical and preoccupied with discovery, not paying attention to project time constraints and relationships. They can deteriorate into arrogance and noncommunication, intellectual bickering, and one-upmanship. At their best, Fives are visionary pioneers, bringing strikingly new ideas and profound depth to their work.
Type Six **The Troubleshooter**	The engaging, loyal type. Likable, responsible, anxious, and suspicious. Sixes are diligent and reliable workers. They build alliances and partnerships that help orient their coworkers and get things done. They are able to assess the motivations and relative merits of others and scan the business environment for potential problems. They dislike taking risks and want consensus and predictability. They can be indecisive and have difficulty taking responsibility or action without group authority and can deteriorate into evasiveness and blaming others. At their best, Sixes are self-reliant, independent, and courageous, often calling a group back to its root values.

Type Seven **The Enthusiast**	The accomplished, upbeat type. Spontaneous, versatile, impulsive, and scattered. Sevens thrive on change, variety, excitement, and innovation. Often articulate and humorous, they are able to get others to support their ideas. They are in touch with the latest trends and are constantly looking for new possibilities and options. They are natural multitaskers but can also get overextended and lack follow-through. They can deteriorate into endless talk and distractions, scattering their energy and talents and leaving many projects unfinished. At their best, Sevens focus on worthwhile goals and become highly productive and accomplished.
Type Eight **The Challenger**	The powerful, decisive type. Self-confident, commanding, willful, and confrontational. Eights have a clear vision of what they want to accomplish and the willpower to make it happen. They make difficult decisions and see serious problems simply as challenges to be met, obstacles to be overcome. They want to be in control and find it difficult to delegate tasks or share leadership. They champion people, protecting and empowering them, but also can deteriorate into intimidation to get their way, making unnecessary enemies both within and outside the organization. At their best, they are magnanimous and generous, using their strength to improve others' lives.
Type Nine **The Peacemaker**	The easygoing, accommodating type. Receptive, reassuring, agreeable, and complacent. Nines create harmony among group members by emphasizing the positive so that conflicts and tensions can be eased. They are supportive and inclusive and work with everyone, humbly allowing others to shine. They dislike conflict and division in the team and try to create harmony and stability. But they may accommodate others and avoid self-assertion too much, becoming secretly angry as a re-

sult. They can deteriorate into ineffectual "make-work," stubborn passivity, and serious neglect. At their best, they are able to negotiate differences and bring people together in a stable but dynamic way.

For more information about business applications, see our Web site at www.EnneagramInstitute.com.

In Relationships

One of the main facts of life that we all have to learn is that *our happiness depends on the quality of our relationships*. We do not thrive in isolation. Having good relationships with intimates, friends, family, and coworkers — with everyone we meet and interact with — is necessary if we are to be happy and fulfilled.

Our relationships are also a bellwether of our emotional and spiritual health: the degree to which we can have healthy, growing relationships mirrors the degree of our psychological functioning as well as our spiritual maturity. It is very difficult for a demanding, fearful, grasping person to have satisfying relationships, whereas a gracious, accepting, and compassionate person most often does. Our own Level of Development (which measures our degree of awareness, nonattachment, and freedom from destructive reactions) is the surest gauge of our ability to have and sustain relationships — and to give as well as receive in them.

The Enneagram can help us become much clearer about our relationship values, expectations, communication and argument styles, thinking and decision patterns, ways of resolving conflicts, fears, defenses, and various coping mechanisms — to name just a few of the elements that affect relationships. These apply to marriage, friendships, and professional relationships — to all kinds of interactions. Each personality type thinks differently, has different values and approaches, and wants different things in a relationship. Furthermore, beginning in the *average* Levels, each type has its own set of issues that make compatibility with other types either more or less difficult. The compatibility strengths and weaknesses for all forty-five combinations of types can be described for each (for example, we can talk about what issues Fours and Ones will have, as well as those for Fours and Twos, Fours and Threes, and so forth for all type combinations).

Good relationships depend on our being able to understand ourselves and others, to see our own needs and the needs of others, and to accept the legitimacy of others' viewpoints while expressing our own. In short, we must be able to treat others as we wish to be treated, even if we have not been treated so well in the past ourselves. Our relationships therefore become the opportunity to revisit the past and to transform ourselves according to more conscious choices in the present.

What Each Type Looks for in a Relationship — and What Interferes

Type One	Shared purpose and values, equality, fairness, integrity. What gets in the way: Insisting on being right at the expense of their connection with the other. Manipulates by correcting others and by playing on their sense of guilt and inadequacy.
Type Two	Emotional connection, intimacy, warmth, affection. What gets in the way: Insisting on exclusivity and ever more closeness. Manipulates by finding out others' needs and desires and by creating secret dependencies.
Type Three	Social suitability, competence, admirability, attractiveness. What gets in the way: Insisting on career and social status before the relationship. Manipulates by charming others and by adopting whatever image will work.
Type Four	Communication, listening, acceptance, emotional honesty. What gets in the way: Insisting on having all of their emotional needs met immediately. Manipulates by being temperamental and making others "walk on eggshells."

Type Five   Curiosity, intensity, involvement, nonintrusiveness. What gets in the way: Insisting on personal space and noninterference. Manipulates by staying preoccupied with ideas and projects and by detaching emotionally from others.

Type Six   Commitment, dependability, shared values, solidity. What gets in the way: Self-doubt and reactivity; vacillating between need for closeness and need for distance. Manipulates by complaining and by testing others' commitment to them.

Type Seven   Stimulation, adventure, excitement, variety. What gets in the way: Insisting on postponing making commitments. Manipulates by staying upbeat and hyperactive and by insisting that others meet their demands for gratification.

Type Eight   Dependability, loyalty, strength, sexual compatibility. What gets in the way: Insisting on maintaining control of others. Manipulates by dominating others and by demanding that others do as they say.

Type Nine   Comfort, peace, harmony, stability. What gets in the way: Insisting on not acknowledging problems and remaining neutral in conflicts. Manipulates by "checking out" and by passive-aggressively resisting others.

For more on relationships, including descriptions of the forty-five type compatibilities, see our Web site at www.EnneagramInstitute.com.

In Parenting

What needs to be said right away in any discussion of parenting is that *parents do not create a child's personality type.* All Enneagram teachers and researchers agree that personality type is built on temperament and that, in ways we do not fully understand, this is inborn. A child comes into the world with his or her personality type already determined by prenatal events, although we do not know what all of these are. There are theories that type is determined by genetics, by *in utero* events, by the emotional state of the mother, or even by past lives and the need for a soul to be a certain type to learn the lessons of that type. But the truth is, we really do not know all of the causes of type.

This is not to say that early family conditions and parental influences are not important: far from it. While they do not cause type, they highly influence how emotionally healthy or unhealthy a child becomes. A child who is fortunate enough to be born into a family of well-balanced parents will start life as a relatively healthy example of his or her type. Conversely, a child who is born into a relatively dysfunctional family will have to close down his natural openness, spontaneity, and vitality and need to erect defenses against the various forms of violation that exist in the family. In the authors' terms, one child will be at a healthier Level of Development, while the second child will grow up at a substantially lower, unhealthier Level. Hence, the second child will have more emotional challenges than the first child.

In short, *parenting does count* — not to produce a personality type, but to influence how healthy a child of that type will be. It is therefore not difficult to see that when parents work on themselves through psychospiritual tools such as the Enneagram, they are not only doing something good for themselves, they are making possible one of the greatest gifts they could give their children — an emotionally healthy childhood and a happier future. Parents who help their child develop self-esteem, emotional stability, open curiosity, trust in self, an enjoyment of life, strength and self-confidence, easiness with themselves, the ability to regulate themselves, and empathy for self and others (qualities found in the nine types) set the stage for the development of all of their child's potentials and future accomplishments.

One of the most useful areas for parents to become aware of is the *differences of fit* between themselves and their children. Not every child will be an easy fit for every parent. If two parents are highly energetic, sociable, and extroverted and their child is quiet, serious, and reserved, the fit between the parents and the child can become strained. The child may unconsciously feel that he or she is a disappointment to the parents, which can cause serious emotional difficulties for the child. The parents might try to manipulate or pressure the child to be more like them. Or they might feel guilty or inadequate for not understanding their child — or even for not completely liking and enjoying their child.

Differences of fit between parents and children can become more clearly understood with the Enneagram. This is not to say that understanding alone will be enough to undo any potential problems. But without insight and understanding there can be no solution to problems. Above all, parents need to see their children not as possessions to be molded according to their own emotional needs but as independent beings who have their own value and are worthy of being treated with dignity and respect.

The following chart indicates a few of the major expectations of each type of parent toward their children, no matter what type their children may actually be. Being aware of these unconscious expectations and not allowing yourself to manipulate your children into having to measure up to them will go a long way toward improving parent-child relationships.

What Parents Expect from Their Children

Type One	May demand self-control, reasonableness, regularity, and the ability to delay rewards — that their child be a Little Adult
Type Two	May demand generosity, thoughtfulness, helpfulness, and attention to others — that their child be a Little Helper
Type Three	May demand being outstanding at tasks, fulfilling family hopes, physical perfection, and popularity — that their child be a Little Superstar
Type Four	May demand sensitivity, artistic creativity, emotional depth, and understanding — that their child be a Little Therapist

Type Five	May demand independence, studiousness, intellectual gifts, and curiosity — that their child be a Little Genius
Type Six	May demand dependability, obedience, perseverance, and trustworthiness — that their child be a Little Trouper
Type Seven	May demand vitality, good humor, resilience, and spontaneity — that their child be a Little Entertainer
Type Eight	May demand toughness, self-sufficiency, courage, and willpower — that their child be a Little Entrepreneur
Type Nine	May demand quietness, lack of demands, gentleness, and non-neediness — that their child be a Little Angel

One of the best attitudes for parents to have toward their children is *an amazed curiosity* to support the child's own unfolding. In childrearing, only one thing is certain: children will develop in unexpected ways. If parents try to block the child's natural unfolding, they will not succeed. The unfolding will not stop but will merely become distorted and neurotic. It is therefore always best for the parent to observe the child's type (with its innate gifts and capacities) and to *elicit the best aspects of the child's type* rather than try to change him or her into someone fundamentally different from who he or she already is.

In Cultural Studies

People often ask if countries have a particular personality type. (In a similar vein, they ask if companies and organizations have a specific personality style — and if religions do as well.)

The answer to these questions is "Yes, they do" — although unfortunately there is as yet no hard scientific evidence to back up this observation. Researchers will have to sample populations to determine the exact mix of the types in any given group or nationality. Nevertheless, we would *not* expect to find an even spread of the nine types across any population, whether it is the

United States, a business, or your local church. For example, intuitively, it is clear that the population of the United States in 2003 is not made up of 11.1 percent of each of the nine types. Yet it is not clear what the precise composition of the American population is. Field testing with a validated test (such as the RHETI, version 2.5) would have to be done to determine the exact proportions in any large population with some degree of accuracy.

Even if this were done, it would not necessarily mean that the culture of a country would be directly reflected in the personality makeup of its citizens. Culture has deeper roots than the personality types of those who make it up at any given time. For example, if empirical testing were to reveal that in the United States in 2003 there was a predominance of types Six, Nine, and Seven, and that Six was numerically the largest group, this would not necessarily mean that the United States should be characterized as a Six country culturally — although over time it might become so.

Nevertheless, countries do seem to have a dominant personality type (or, perhaps more appropriately, style), although we have observed that, in any country at a given time, *three dominant types* seem to be the main components of the "national character." These three dominant types not only color the personality of the country as a whole, they also change from historical era to historical era. For example, we think that culturally the United States in 2003 is predominantly a Three, Six, and Seven country. This means that we see the Three's drive for success, fame, status, narcissism, and concern for image and career, major themes in the current American character. This is joined by the Seven's love of the new and immediate, high energy, love of change and variety, and insatiable consumerism. Added to these two threads are the Six's traditionalism, conservatism, respect for law, authority and institutions, "family values," and apprehensiveness about the future. These three types (seen metaphorically and psychologically) are the three uppermost elements in the American psyche *at this time*.

From the perspective of the Enneagram, all value sets based on personality needs and biases are equally relative. They all have their positive, enriching aspects as well as their negative, destructive ones. Using the Enneagram to analyze and understand cultural differences may be one of the most important applications of this system for diplomacy and international understanding. After all, one of the messages of the Enneagram is that, fundamentally, we are all alike — all of us are human beings who have similar hopes, fears, needs, limitations, and aspirations. Despite cultural differences and historical accidents, we are more similar to each other than we could have imagined. Our belief in the "oneness of humanity" becomes a living perception and the basis for positive action in the world, not merely a fine-sounding but empty phrase. Once the world understands this, the possibility of real peace will become greatly increased.

The following assignment of three personality styles in the national character of several countries is, of course, an educated guess until appropriate empirical research can be done.

The Personality Types (Styles) of Contemporary Countries

England	Types One, Five, and Six
United States	Types Three, Six, and Seven
France	Types Three, Four, and Seven
China	Types Three, Eight, and Nine
Japan	Types Six, Four, and Five
Germany	Types Six, Five, and Eight
Russia	Types Six, Eight, and Four
Italy	Types Eight, Two, and Seven

In Personal Growth

We must always remember that the primary use for the Enneagram is for self-discovery and personal growth. The Enneagram helps bring to light what was formerly hidden from us — to "make the unconscious conscious," as Freud put it. From a spiritual perspective, the purpose of the Enneagram is to point out to us the patterns of distortions and illusions that we mistakenly take to be ourselves. It is a tool for self-realization and self-actualization — for clarifying our psyche so that it can be given up in a surrender to the Divine.

The nine types are detailed reminders of our "waking sleep" (as Gurdjieff taught), of "who we are not," rather than identities that cause further attachment to our egos and the perpetuation of our illusions and sufferings. As such, the personality types are really catalogues of our own particular case of mistaken identity, and they contain a considerable amount of bad news for our egos. But if we look deeper, we can also see that there is in the Enneagram an implied invitation to stop our self-destructive patterns by seeing them more objectively and compassionately. Our waking up is the beginning of the process of transformation.

Each Type's Wake-Up Call and Movement Toward Liberation

Type One — Awareness of feeling a sense of personal obligation to fix everything themselves — so that they can rise to a profound acceptance of and genuine tolerance for reality.

Type Two — Awareness of believing that they must go out to others to win them over — so that they can rise to unconditional love of self and others, irrespective of others' reactions to them.

Type Three — Awareness of always driving themselves to be the best and to get validation — so that they can rise to genuine embodiment of real values and an authentic expression of who they really are.

Type Four — Awareness of holding on to and intensifying feelings through the imagination — so that they can rise to a self-regenerating connection with reality and endless creativity.

Type Five — Awareness of withdrawing from reality into concepts and mental worlds — so that they can rise to a profound and objective understanding of how reality really is.

Type Six — Awareness of becoming dependent on something outside the self for guidance — so that they can rise to be-

come grounded in their own inner guidance and feeling
of endless support.

Type Seven   Awareness of feeling that "something better" is available somewhere else — so that they can rise to a true
resting in the moment and a joyous celebration of life.

Type Eight   Awareness of feeling that they must push and struggle
to make things happen — so that they can rise to a true
self-surrender to something greater and more lasting
than themselves.

Type Nine   Awareness of the tendency to accommodate themselves
outwardly to others — so that they can rise to a genuine
remembering of themselves and their own strength,
value, and dignity.

The Enneagram helps us take concrete steps toward recovering
our True Nature, our spiritual selves. But even the most dedicated
spiritual seekers generally do not go from a genuine spiritual realization to a permanent transformation without a lot of significant
Inner Work over a long period of time. Old patterns of behavior,
beliefs, attitudes, values, defenses — and much else — must be
exposed and clarified in our psyches. This is not a short, all-at-
once process, and one encounters many obstacles and paradoxes
along the way.

Yet here again the Enneagram can help to make traveling the
path of self-knowledge surer. By exposing the psychospiritual obstacles presented by our type, it makes working with them
clearer, especially if we see them in a larger context. By reminding
us to bring awareness to the moment, it helps us see our behaviors
and motivations, fears and desires, attitudes and defenses *in action.* By observing ourselves in the moment, we learn to reverse
the hidden self-defeating mechanisms of our type. By fully acknowledging and staying present to our fears, hurts, and cravings
without acting them out or repressing them, we discover who we
really are and find our inner strength — and a way out of our problems.

If we stay awake to our inner states, even to our suffering, quite miraculously, things begin to shift. We find that life becomes easier, because we can use our time and energy for living creatively rather than wasting them on internal turmoil and conflicts. We also discover that, once our unconscious, automatic patterns start dropping away, we become free of older, limiting identities. We then naturally find ourselves drawn to healthier ways of living and relating — and to a felt sense of our own dignity and the dignity of others.

As we move into a new millennium, we recognize more than ever *the vital importance of waking up.* By this, we mean not only waking up to the truth of what our personality is up to, but just as important, waking up to the majesty of our depths, to the riches of the spirit. For real change to occur in the world and for human beings to discover their common humanity, there must be real transformation first in each individual so that we can become vehicles of Consciousness. Only by more human beings becoming more deeply conscious will we escape from our self-destructive impulses. This can only happen one person at a time, beginning with ourselves, here and now.

Appendix:
The Validation of the RHETI

In March, 2001, the *Riso-Hudson Enneagram Type Indicator* (RHETI, version 2.5) was officially validated by independent research, a doctoral dissertation written by Rebecca Newgent, Ph.D., at the University of Akron. Dr. Newgent's dissertation is entitled *An Investigation of the Reliability and Validity of the Riso-Hudson Enneagram Type Indicator* and is available from UMI Dissertation Services (at 800-521-0600). Dr. Newgent concluded that the RHETI is scientifically "valid and reliable" as a test instrument with "solid psychometrics." With these findings, the RHETI becomes the most widely used Enneagram-based questionnaire to be independently validated by an impartial researcher.

Internal-consistency reliability scores indicate that the RHETI ranges from 56 percent to 82 percent accurate on the various types, with an overall accuracy of 72 percent. These scores are the result of "blind testing." Neither the instructor nor the test takers had any Enneagram instruction, so these scores would be expected to be significantly higher after more exposure to the Enneagram. Nevertheless, this is quite respectable for a psychological test and compares favorably with other Enneagram-based tests. Additional research is planned to bring the RHETI more solidly into the 80 percent range overall, which would be an extraordinarily high rating for a psychological test based on self-reportage.

According to this research on the RHETI, the internal-consistency reliability alpha (Cronbach Coefficient Alpha) scores for the nine types of the Enneagram as measured by the RHETI are as follows:

Type One: 73 percent
Type Two: 82 percent
Type Three: 56 percent
Type Four: 70 percent
Type Five: 56 percent
Type Six: 66 percent
Type Seven: 80 percent
Type Eight: 75 percent
Type Nine: 79 percent

Dr. Newgent also compared the RHETI with the NEO PI-R test, which has become the psychometric standard for testing nonpathological personality. The NEO PI-R measures the factors of Neuroticism, Extraversion, Openness, Agreeableness, and Conscientiousness (the "Five Factor Model"). According to Dr. Newgent, "results of testing . . . indicated strong correlations between the findings of the RHETI and the factors of the NEO-PI-R."

Dr. Newgent further found that "results of testing for concurrent validity between the RHETI types and the NEO PI-R factors indicate that the majority of the demographic descriptive variables are invariant to the RHETI. The RHETI was able to predict the NEO PI-R factors a majority of the time, with a few exceptions, regardless of the demographic variable."

Drafting and pretesting on the RHETI began in 1993. The authors hope that the RHETI, independently researched at this high level of validation, will give more credibility to the Enneagram in academic, educational, and business fields. (Qualified researchers are invited to contact The Enneagram Institute to undertake further research on the RHETI and/or other aspects of the authors' work with the Enneagram.) The results of Dr. Newgent's research also indirectly indicate the solid grounding of the Insight Approach℠ on which the RHETI is based. This test could not have been constructed without careful observation of individuals, precision in discriminating differences between the types, and the conceptual underpinning of the RHETI with the Levels of Development, as well as other factors that are part of the Insight Approach.

Resources

Books

Almaas, A. H. *Diamond Heart (Vols. 1–1V)*. Boston and London: Shambala, 1987–1997.

———. *Essence*. York Beach, Maine: Samuel Weiser, 1986.

———. *Spacecruiser Inquiry*. Boston and London: Shambala, 2002.

Epstein, Mark. *Thoughts Without a Thinker*. New York: Basic, 1995.

Horney, Karen. *Neurosis and Human Growth*. New York: W. W. Norton, 1950.

———. *Our Inner Conflicts*. New York: W. W. Norton, 1945.

Kornfield, Jack. *A Path with Heart*. New York: Bantam, 1993.

Mitchell, Stephen A., and Margaret J. Black. *Freud and Beyond*. New York: Basic, 1995.

Naranjo, Claudio. *Character and Neurosis*. Nevada City, Calif.: Gateways/IDHHB, 1994.

Nisargadatta, Maharaj. *I Am That*. Translated by Maurice Frydman. Durham, N.C.: Acorn, 1973, 1982.

Ouspensky, P. D. *In Search of the Miraculous*. New York: Harcourt, Brace & World, 1949.

———. *The Fourth Way*. New York: Vintage, 1957, 1971.

Riso, Don Richard. *Enneagram Transformations*. Boston: Houghton Mifflin, 1993.

Riso, Don Richard, and Russ Hudson. *Understanding the Enneagram*. Boston: Houghton Mifflin, 1990, 2000.

Riso, Don Richard, and Russ Hudson. *The Wisdom of the Enneagram*. New York: Bantam, 1999.

Riso, Don Richard, with Russ Hudson. *Personality Types*. Boston: Houghton Mifflin, 1987, 1996.

Smith, Huston. *Forgotten Truth*. San Francisco: Harper San Francisco, 1985.

Speeth, Kathleen Riordan. *The Gurdjieff Work*. Berkeley, Calif.: And/Or Press, 1976.

211

Tolle, Eckhart. *The Power of Now.* Novato, Calif.: New World Library, 1999.

Walsh, Roger, and Frances Vaughn. *Paths Beyond Ego.* Los Angeles: Jeremy P. Tarcher/Perigee, 1993.

Wilber, Ken. *The Eye of Spirit.* Boston: Shambhala, 1997.

A Note on Enneagram Books

Numerous books on the Enneagram are currently available. Readers have become confused, however, by the inconsistencies and contradictions among them. Enneagram books about relationships, business, spirituality — or about any other topic, for that matter — will be of little use if they are based on an incomplete, anecdote-based notion of the types or of the Enneagram as a whole.

While all books on this field draw on Oscar Ichazo's seminal work in varying degrees, it is important to realize that there are many different teachings and approaches being referred to as "the Enneagram." For better or worse, there is no single authentic approach to the Enneagram — and no official interpretation or teaching method that has come down through history in an "oral tradition" of any kind.

The Enneagram is a work in progress, and its continuing development relies on different authors making continuing discoveries and applications of it. Those interested in this system are therefore urged to read all Enneagram books (including our own) critically, to think for themselves, and always to judge everything by their own experience.

Web Sites

The Enneagram Institute (worldwide organization)

For more information about the Insight Approach[SM] and for a reference to local Riso-Hudson–trained Enneagram teachers in your area, please contact

> Don Richard Riso, President
> Russ Hudson, Executive Director
> 3355 Main Street (Route 209)
> Stone Ridge, NY 12484
> Phone: (845) 687-9878
> Fax: (845) 687-7486
> E-mail: Info@EnneagramInstitute.com
> Web site: www.EnneagramInstitute.com

Faculty of The Enneagram Institute

The name The Enneagram Institute[SM] is service marked and may not be used by individuals or organizations not affiliated directly with The Enneagram Institute of New York.

The Enneagram Institute of New Mexico
>   Brian Grodner, Ph.D.
>   2741 Indian School Rd. NE
>   Albuquerque, NM 87106
>   Phone: (505) 255-6002
>   Fax: (505) 255-7890
>   E-mail: info@DrGrodnerRapidChange.com
>   Web site: www.DrGrodnerRapidChange.com

The Enneagram Institute of Central Ohio
>   Belinda Gore, Ph.D.
>   3105 Waukeegan Avenue
>   Lewis Center, OH 43035
>   Phone: (614) 227-9903
>   Fax: (614) 885-2453
>   E-mail: bgore@enneagram-ohio.com
>   Web site: www.enneagram-ohio.com

The Enneagram Institute of Tampa Bay
>   Jane W. Hollister, Director
>   P.O. Box 17656
>   Tampa, FL 336682-7656
>   Phone and fax: (813) 932-2842
>   E-mail: jaholl@worldnet.att.net

The Enneagram Institute of Colorado
>   Gayle Scott
>   7232 Olde Stage Road
>   Boulder, CO 80302-9411
>   Phone: (303) 545-5767
>   Fax: (303) 545-5765
>   E-mail: gaylescott@aol.com

The Enneagram Institute of Japan
Tim McLean and Yoshiko Takaoka
168-14 Akazawa
Ito-shi, Shizuoka-ken
Japan, 413-0233
Phone and fax: 81-557-54-7522

International Enneagram Association
"We sponsor open and constructive interactions among various schools of Enneagram thought, encourage innovative applications of the Enneagram, and build community through grassroots regional participation."
IEA Headquarters
4100 Executive Park Drive, Suite 16
Cincinnati, OH 45241
Phone: (513) 232-5054
Web site: www.intl-enneagram-assn.org

EnneaMotion
Andrea Isaacs is a Riso-Hudson faculty member and originator of "Ennea-Motion — Transformation Through Movement," now part of a larger body of work called "Physical Intelligence." She is known for her original work exploring the relationship between personality and the body. For more information, contact her at
117 Sweetmilk Creek Road
Center Brunswick, NY 12180
Phone: (518) 279-4444
E-mail: andreais@earthlink.net
Web site: www.physical-intelligence.com

Enneagram Monthly (Newspaper)
748 Wayside Road
Portola Valley, CA 94028
Phone: (650) 851- 4806
Email: EnneaMonth@aol.com
Web site: www.ideodynamic.com/enneagram-monthly

Learn More

The accuracy and usefulness of the material in this book, including the RHETI questionnaire (version 2.5), is made possible by the Insight Approach^{SM} of Don Riso and Russ Hudson. The Insight Approach emphasizes clear and precise understanding of each personality type and the Enneagram system as a whole. The Insight Approach relies on the internal Levels of Development of each type as well as rigorous conceptualization and investigation, individual observation and interviewing, and in-depth understanding and intuition for information about the system.

For the only training program that covers *all* elements of the complete Enneagram system, consider coming to the Riso-Hudson Enneagram Professional Training Program. Don Riso and Russ Hudson offer a comprehensive, three-part Enneagram Professional Training Program each year. The Training is designed to equip serious students of the Enneagram to teach and make applications of the system in areas as diverse as personal growth, business, education, spirituality, relationships, therapy, and counseling. Contact The Enneagram Institute at the address below for more information about the training program.

Don Riso and Russ Hudson also give workshops worldwide on relationships, on inner work with the Enneagram, on the psychic structures and the superego, on business applications, and on other basic and advanced topics.

To contact The Enneagram Institute for information about Riso-Hudson Enneagram trainings and workshops, new publications, business seminars, audiotapes, and other resources, or to have your name added to its mailing list, please contact

The Enneagram Institute
> 3355 Main Street (Route 209)
> Stone Ridge, NY 12484
> Phone: (845) 687-9878
> Fax: (845) 687-7486
> E-mail: Info@EnneagramInstitute.com
> Web site: www:EnneagramInstitute.com

ENNEAGRAM RESOURCES BY DON RICHARD RISO

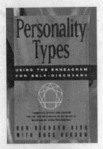

PERSONALITY TYPES
Using the Enneagram for Self-Discovery, revised, with Russ Hudson (1990, 1996) This new edition updates the descriptions of the nine personality types and greatly expands the accompanying guidelines, uncovering the Core Dynamics, or Levels of Development, within each type. ISBN 0-395-79867-1

UNDERSTANDING THE ENNEAGRAM
The Practical Guide to Personality Types, revised, with Russ Hudson (1990, 2000) This authoritative guide to the Enneagram is an indispensable resource that teaches not only how to understand this psychological framework in daily life but how to use it in many different settings. ISBN 0-618-00415-7

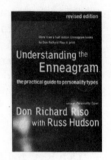

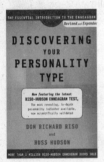

DISCOVERING YOUR PERSONALITY TYPE
The Essential Introduction to the Enneagram, revised and expanded, with Russ Hudson (1995, 2003) The best general introduction to using the Enneagram, this new edition contains a highly accurate personality test that identifies basic personality types to yield a complete psychological profile. Now featuring the Ennea-gram Questionnaire, version 2.5. ISBN 0-618-21903-X

ENNEAGRAM TRANSFORMATIONS
Releases and Affirmations for Healing Your Personality Type (1993) In this groundbreaking work, Riso offers readers the opportunity to take a psychological inventory of inner strengths that can be invaluable for self-development and all forms of recovery. ISBN 0-395-65786-5

 AVAILABLE FROM HOUGHTON MIFFLIN